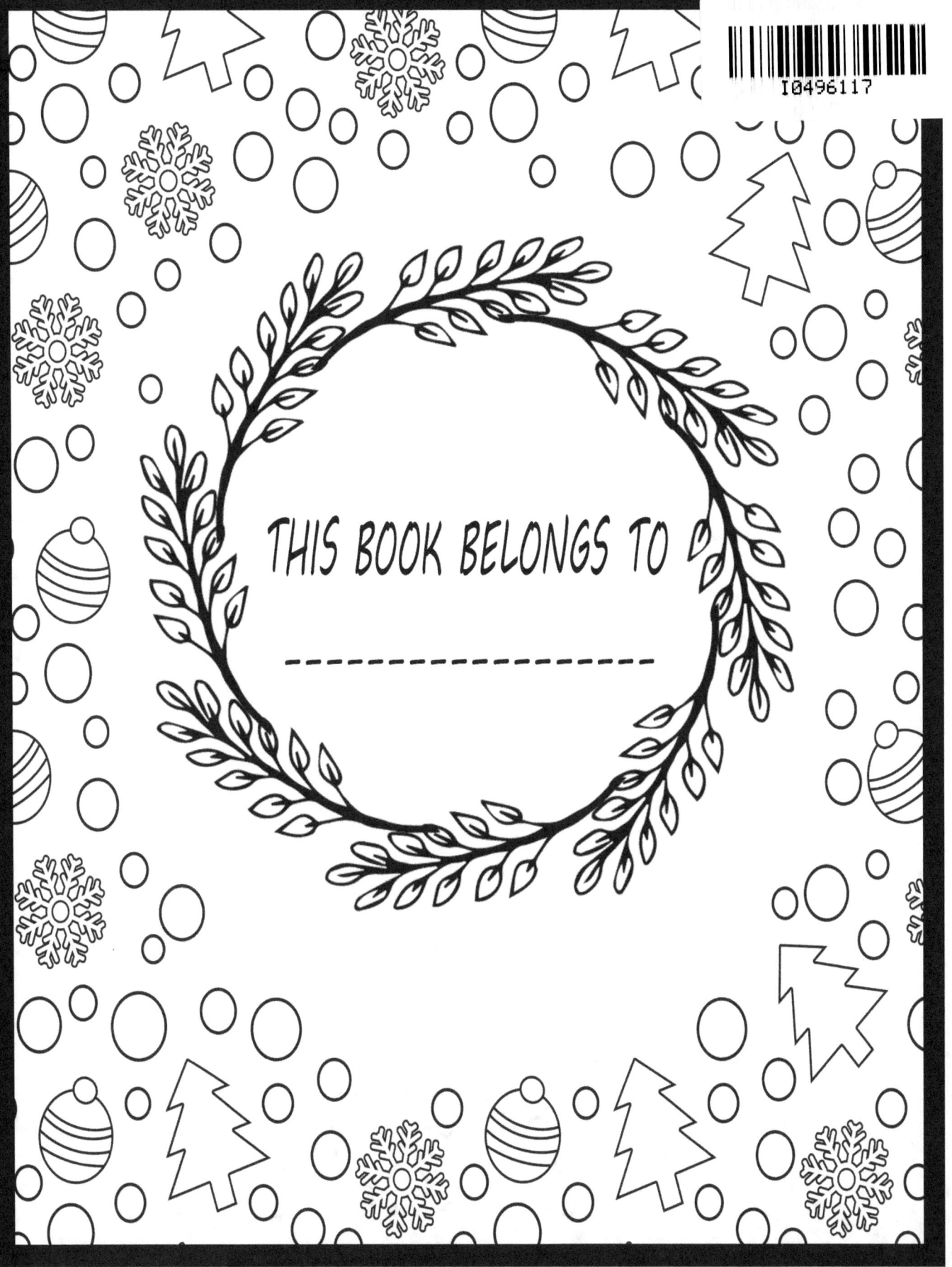

COLORING BOOK

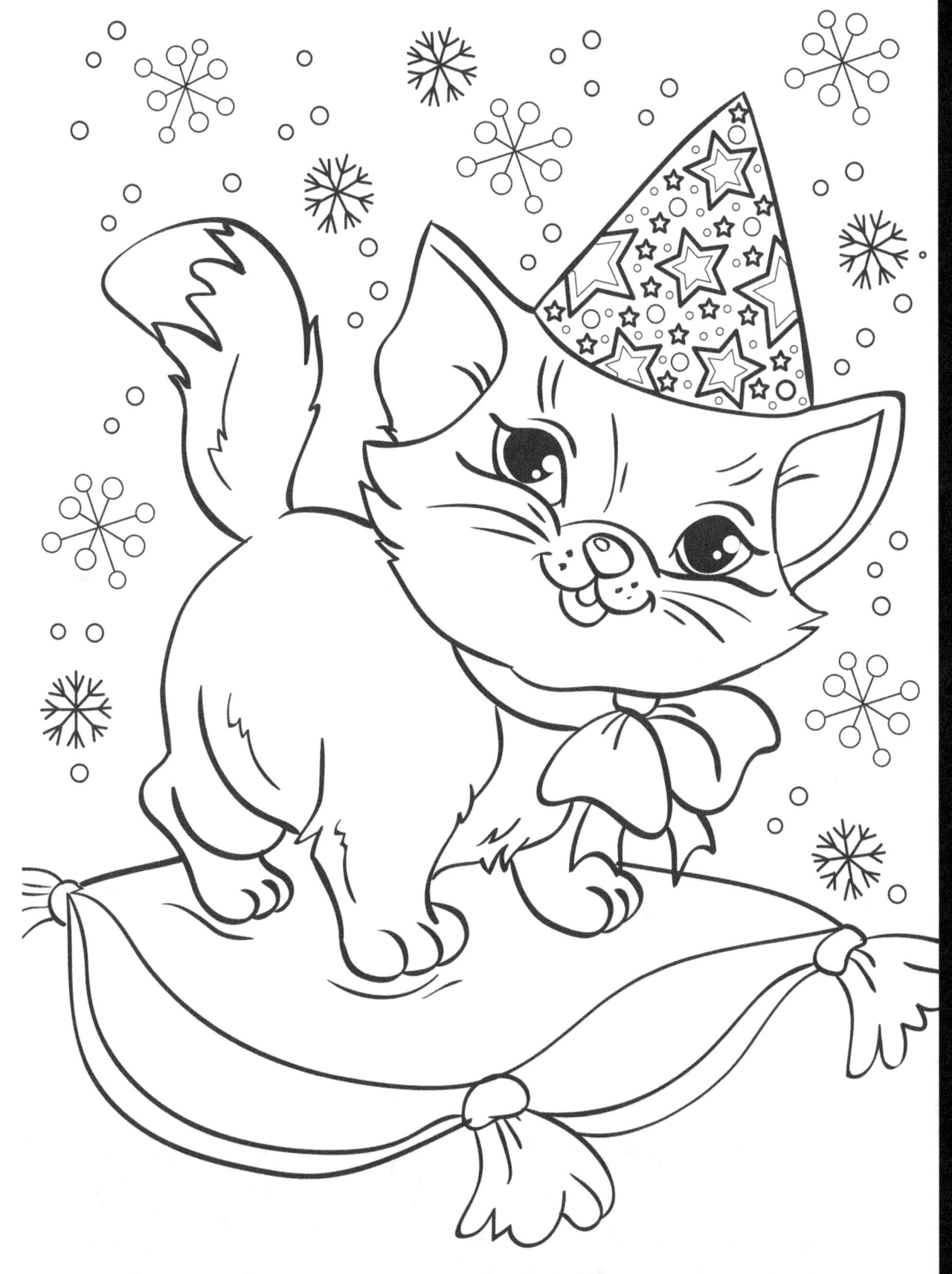

COLORING BOOK

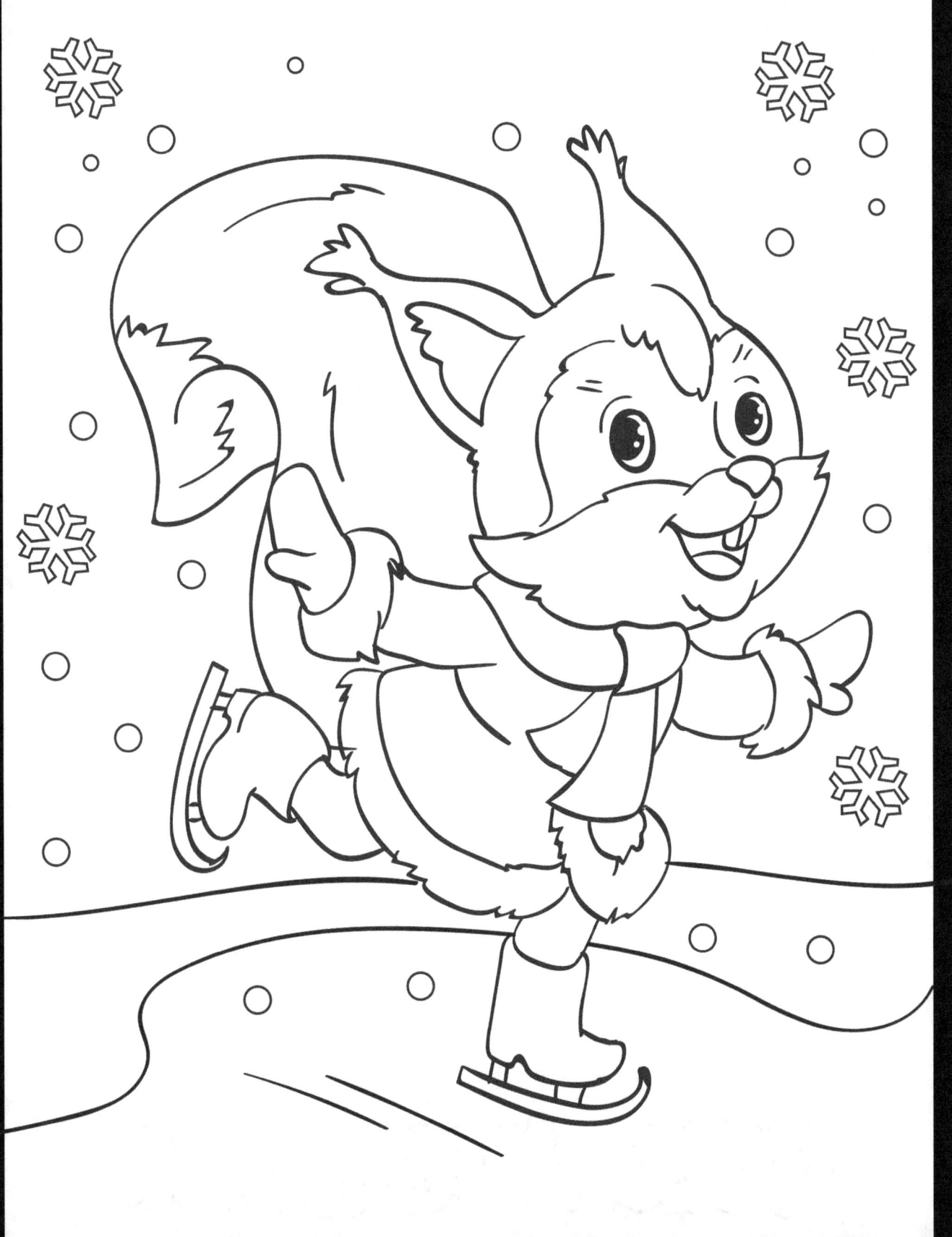

COLORING BOOK

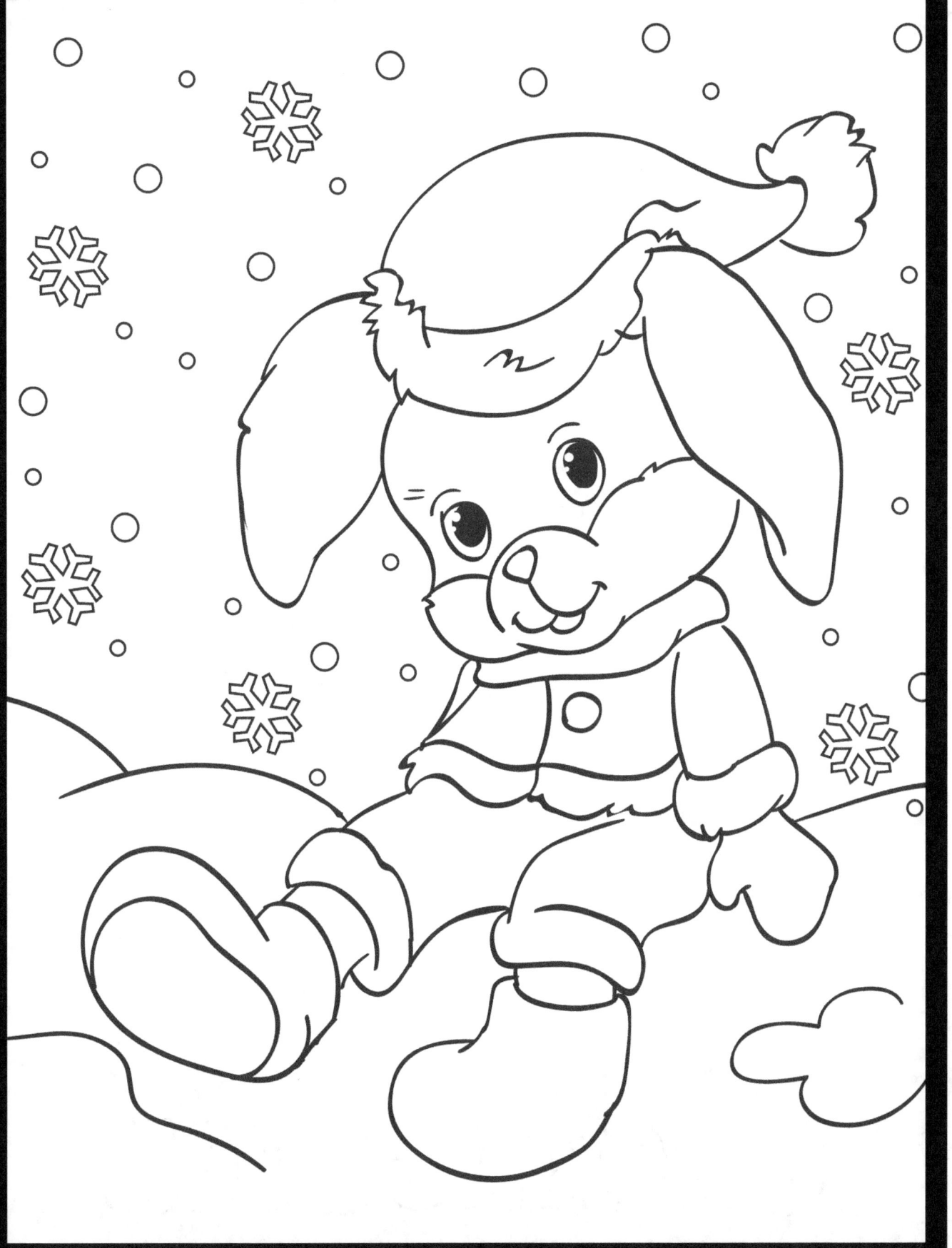

COLORING BOOK

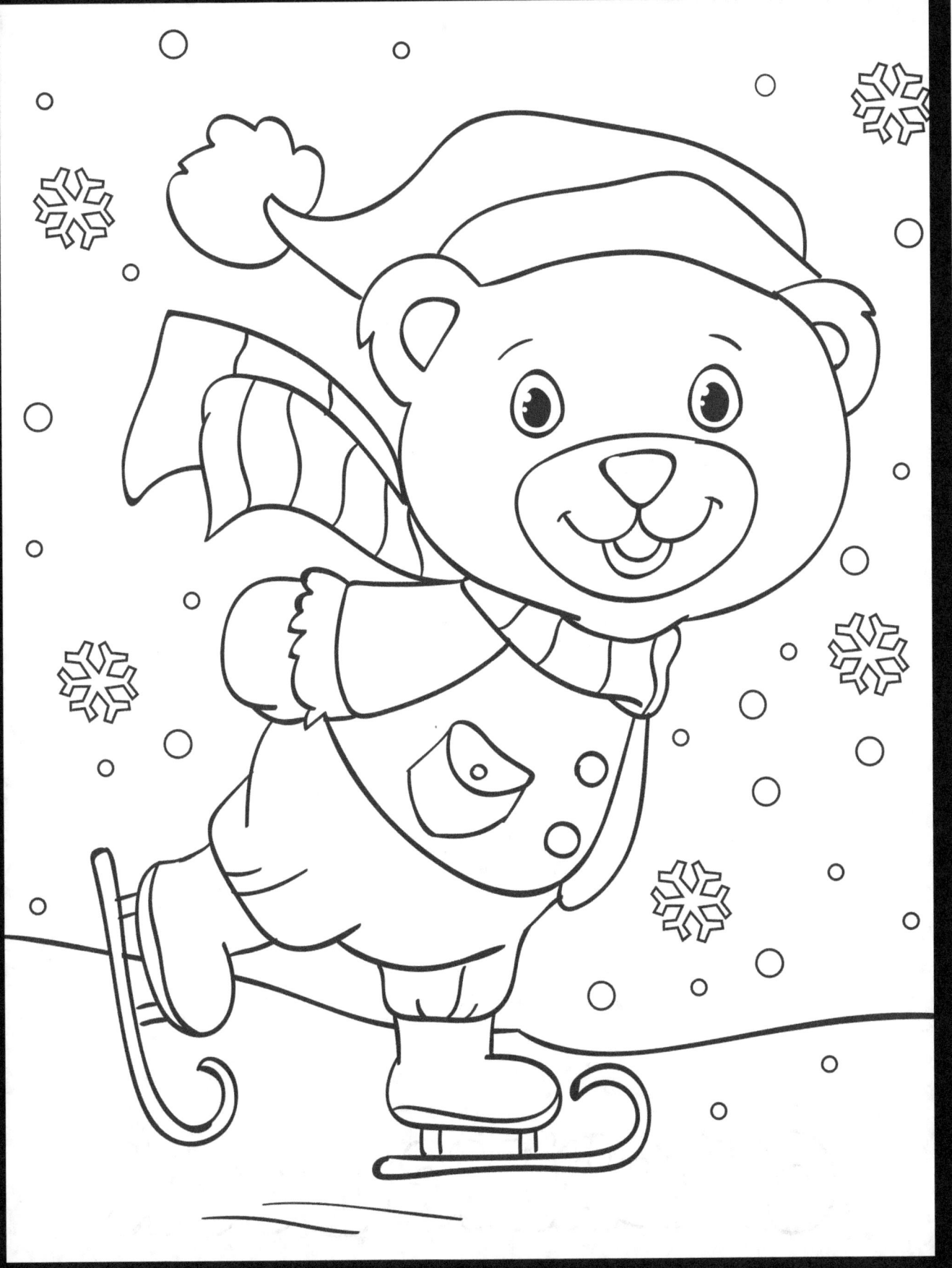

COLORING BOOK

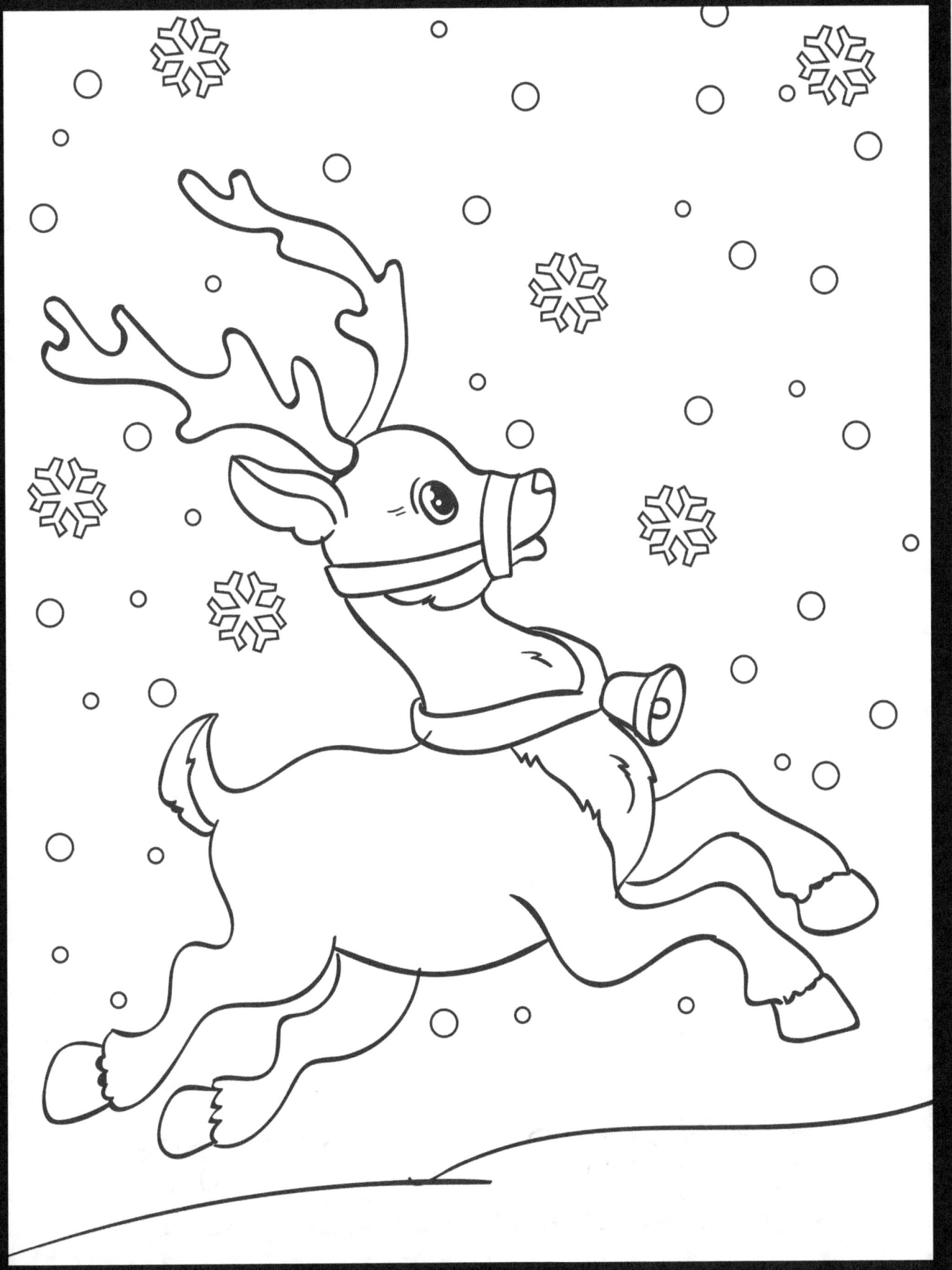

COLORING BOOK

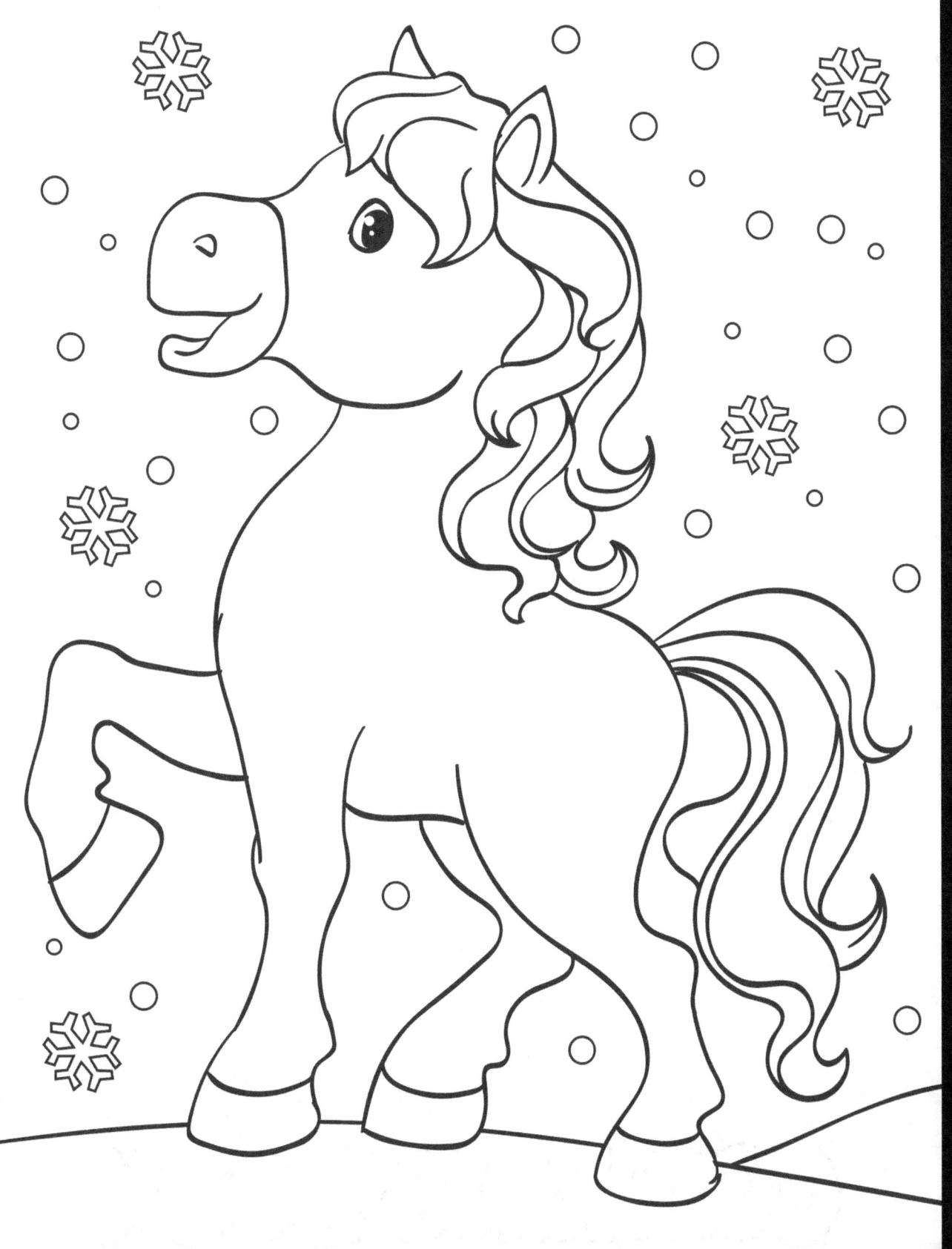

COLORING BOOK

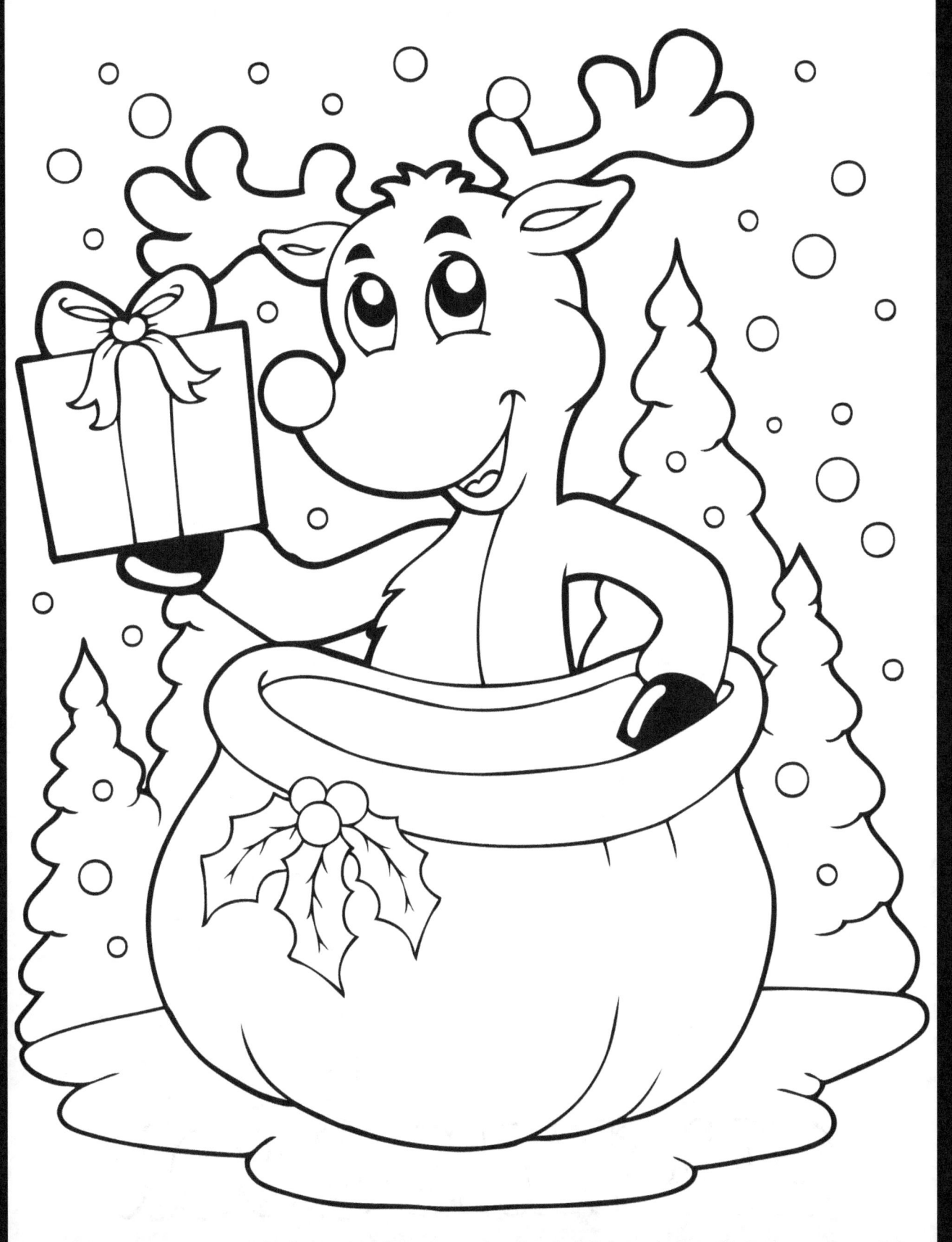

COLORING BOOK

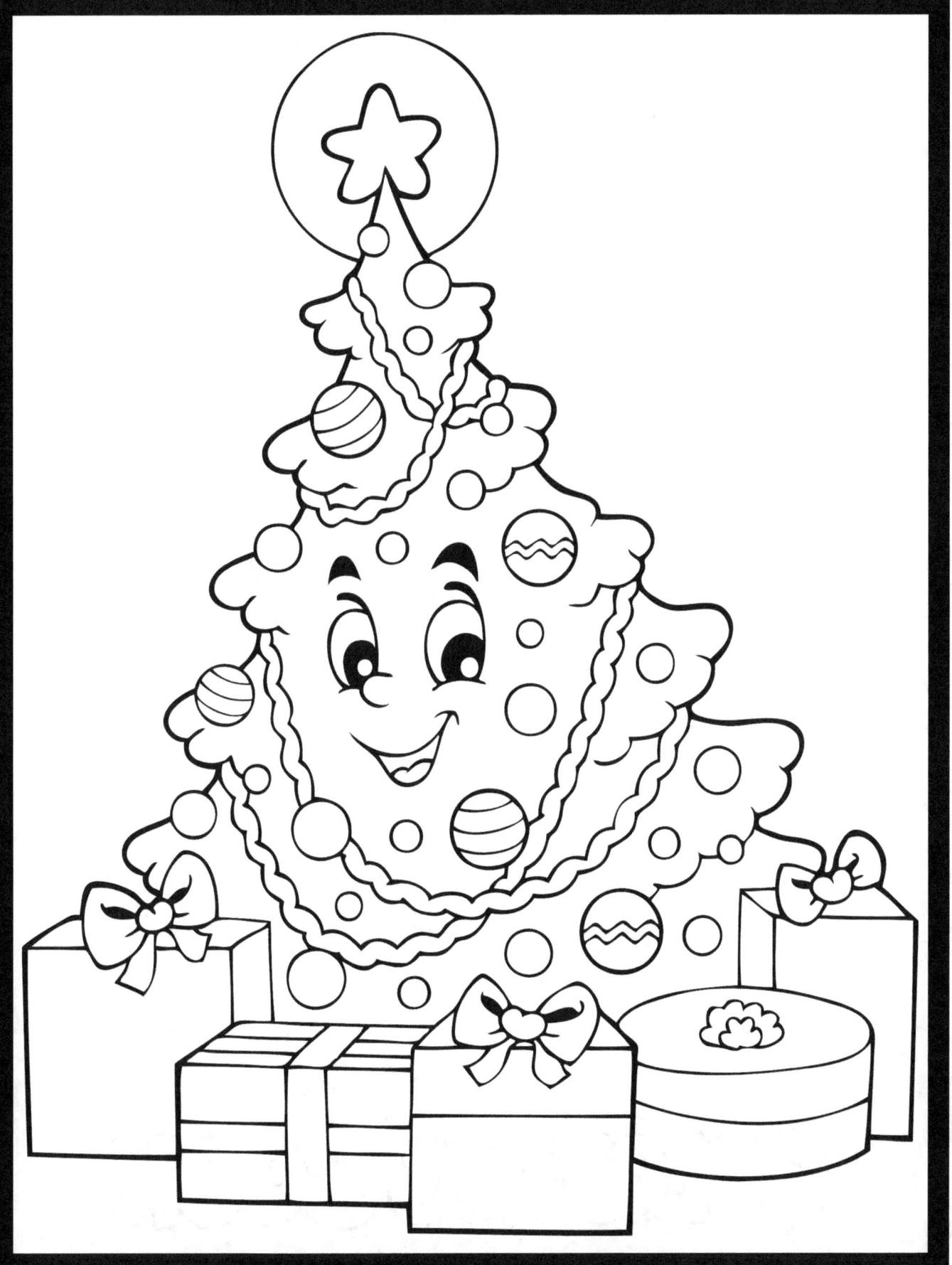

COLORING BOOK

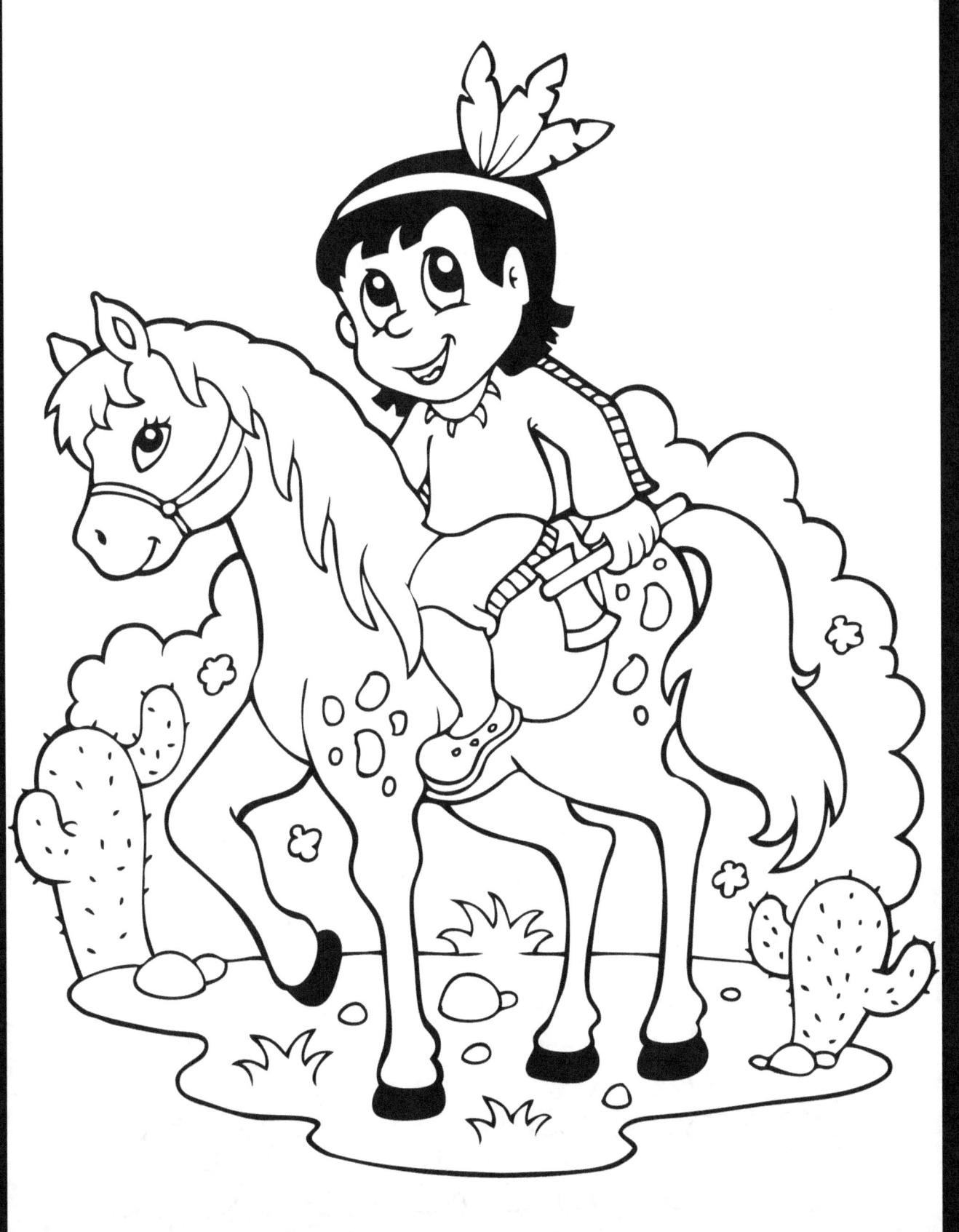

COLORING BOOK

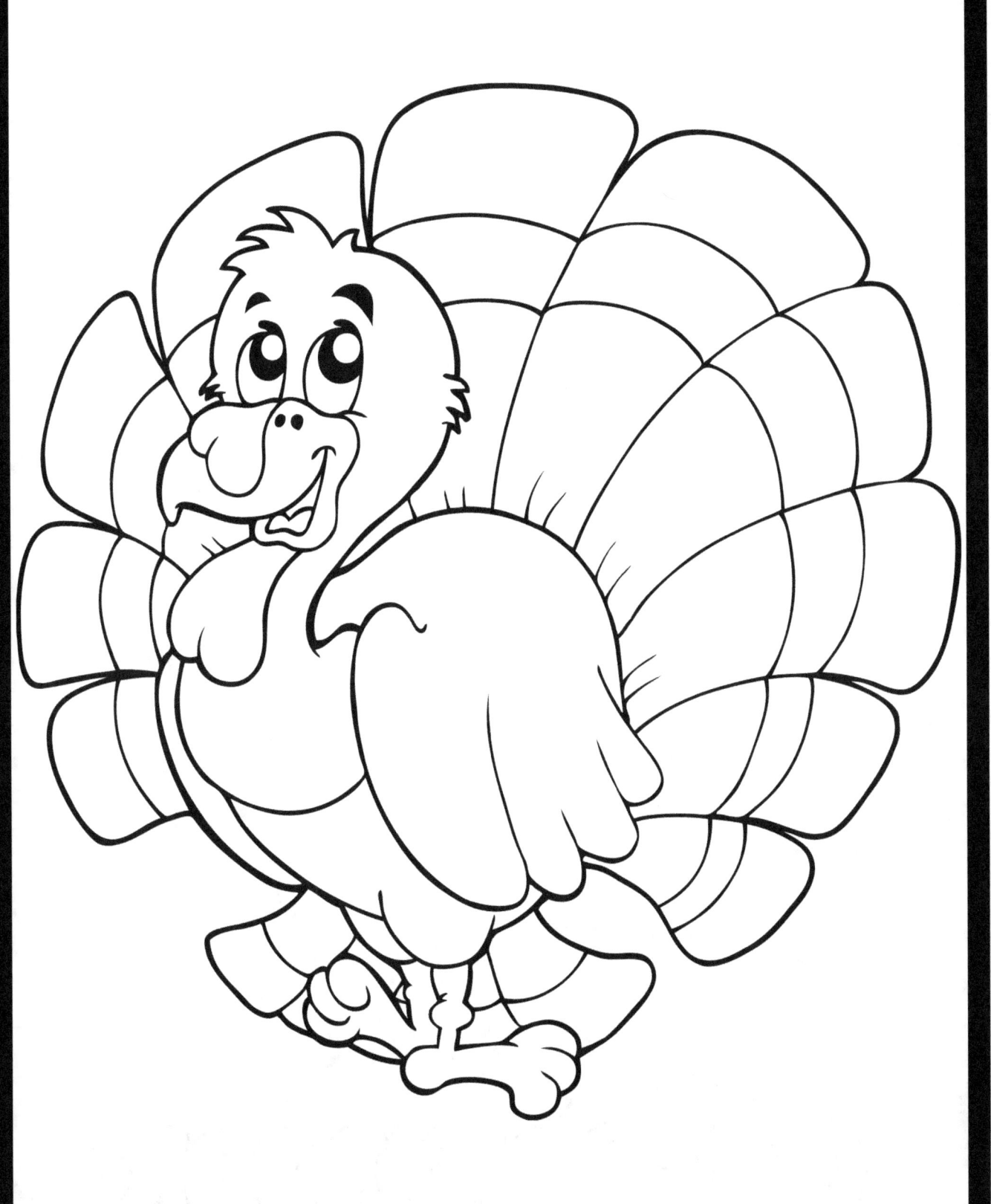

COLORING BOOK

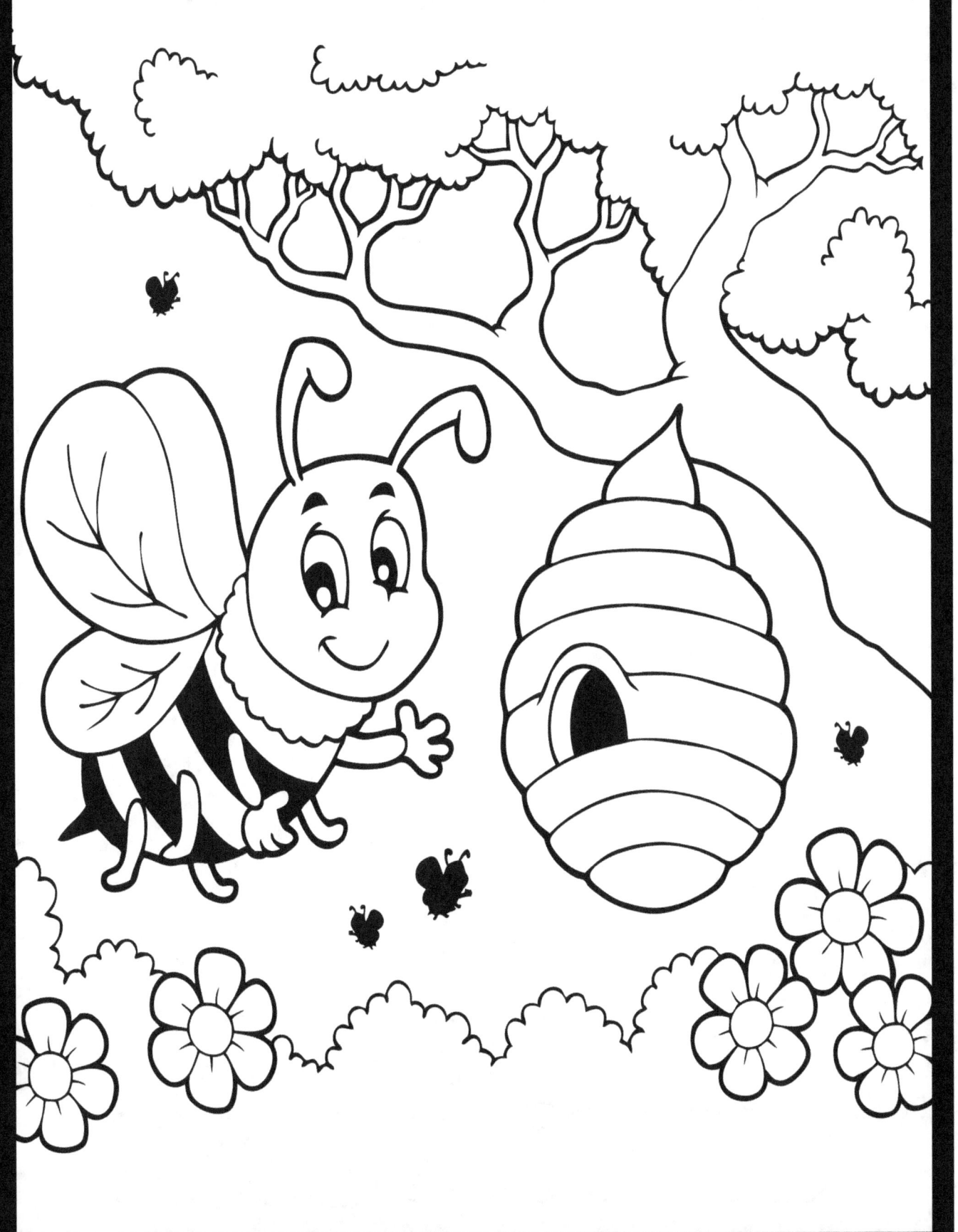

COLORING BOOK

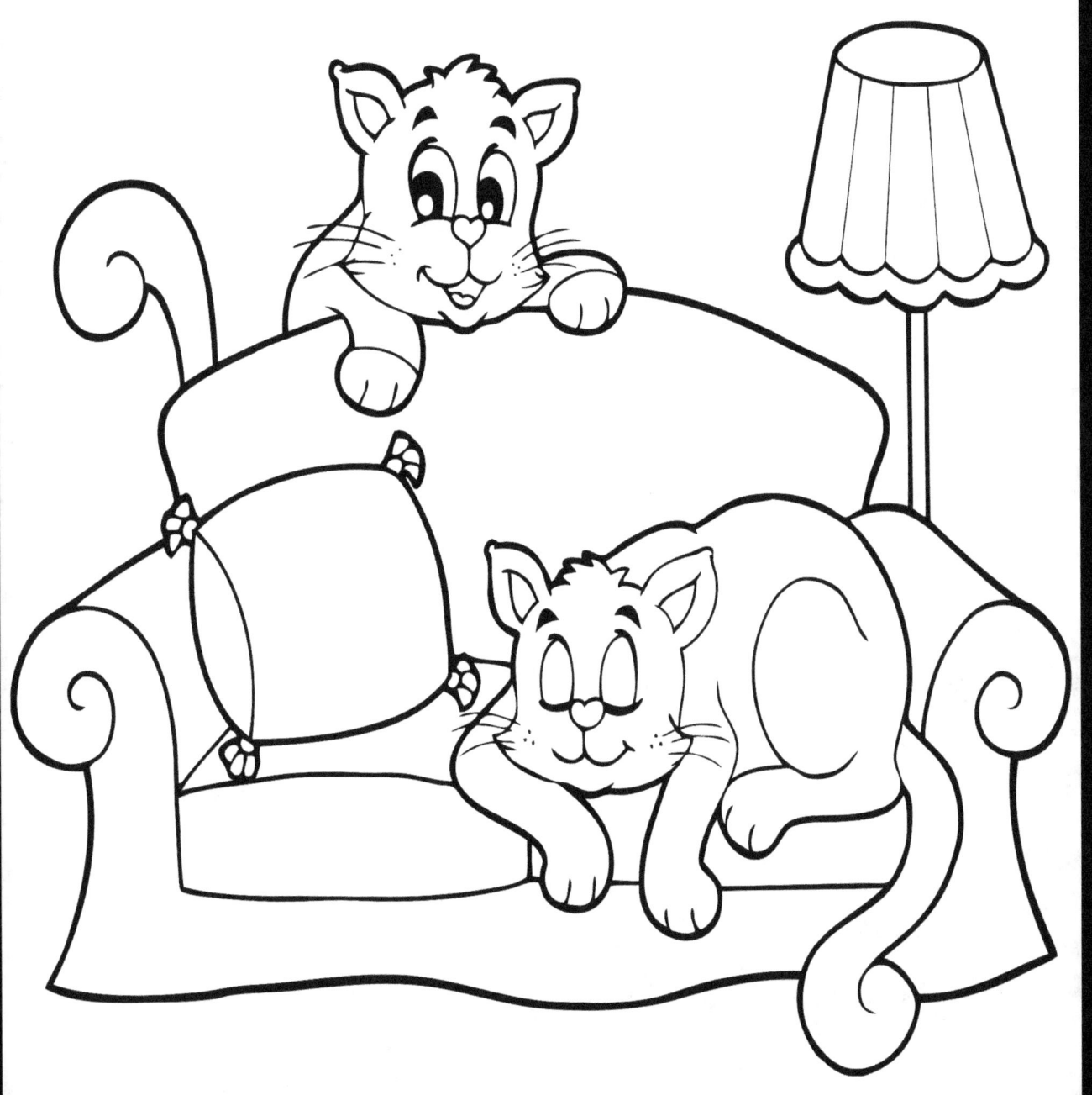

COLORING BOOK

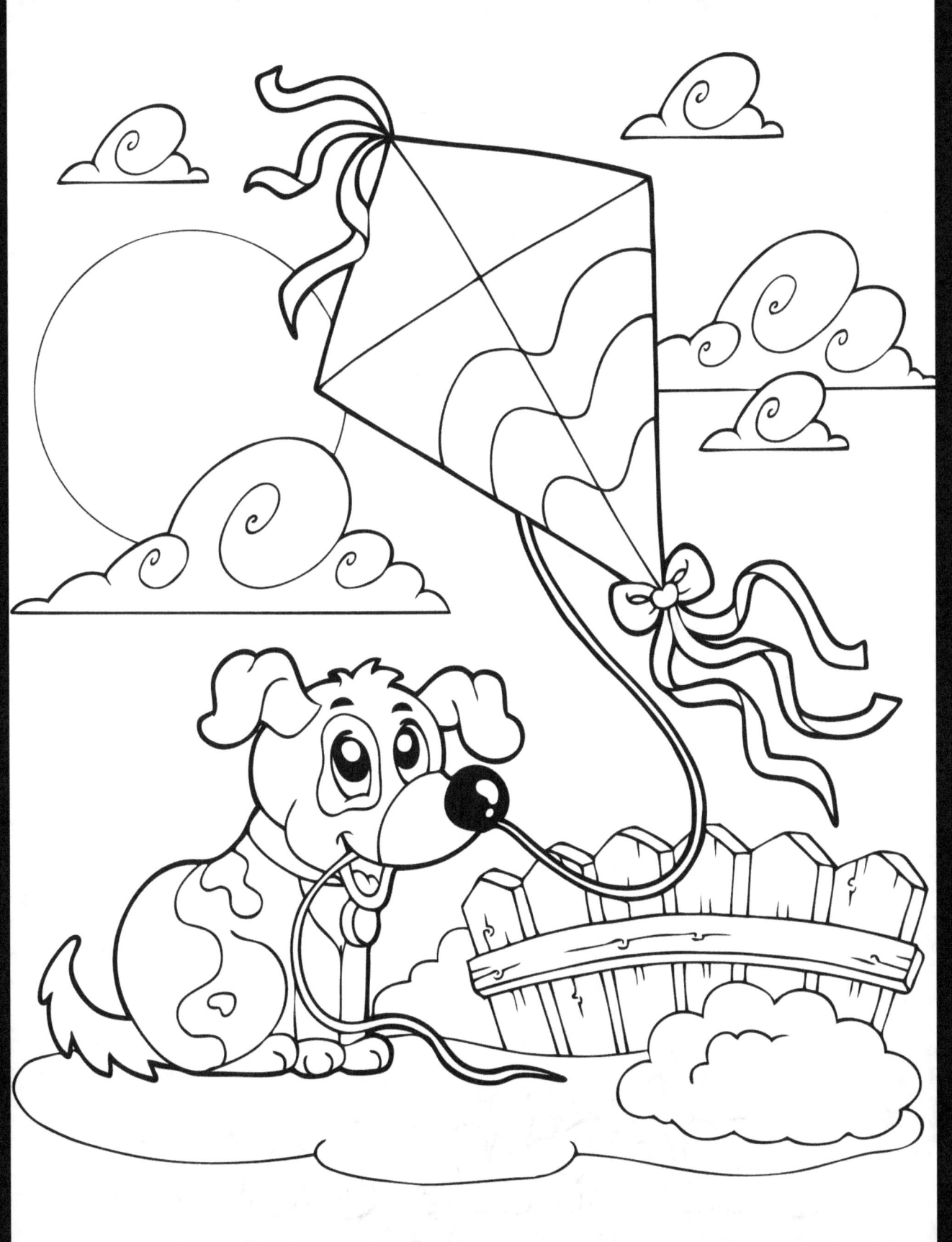

COLORING BOOK

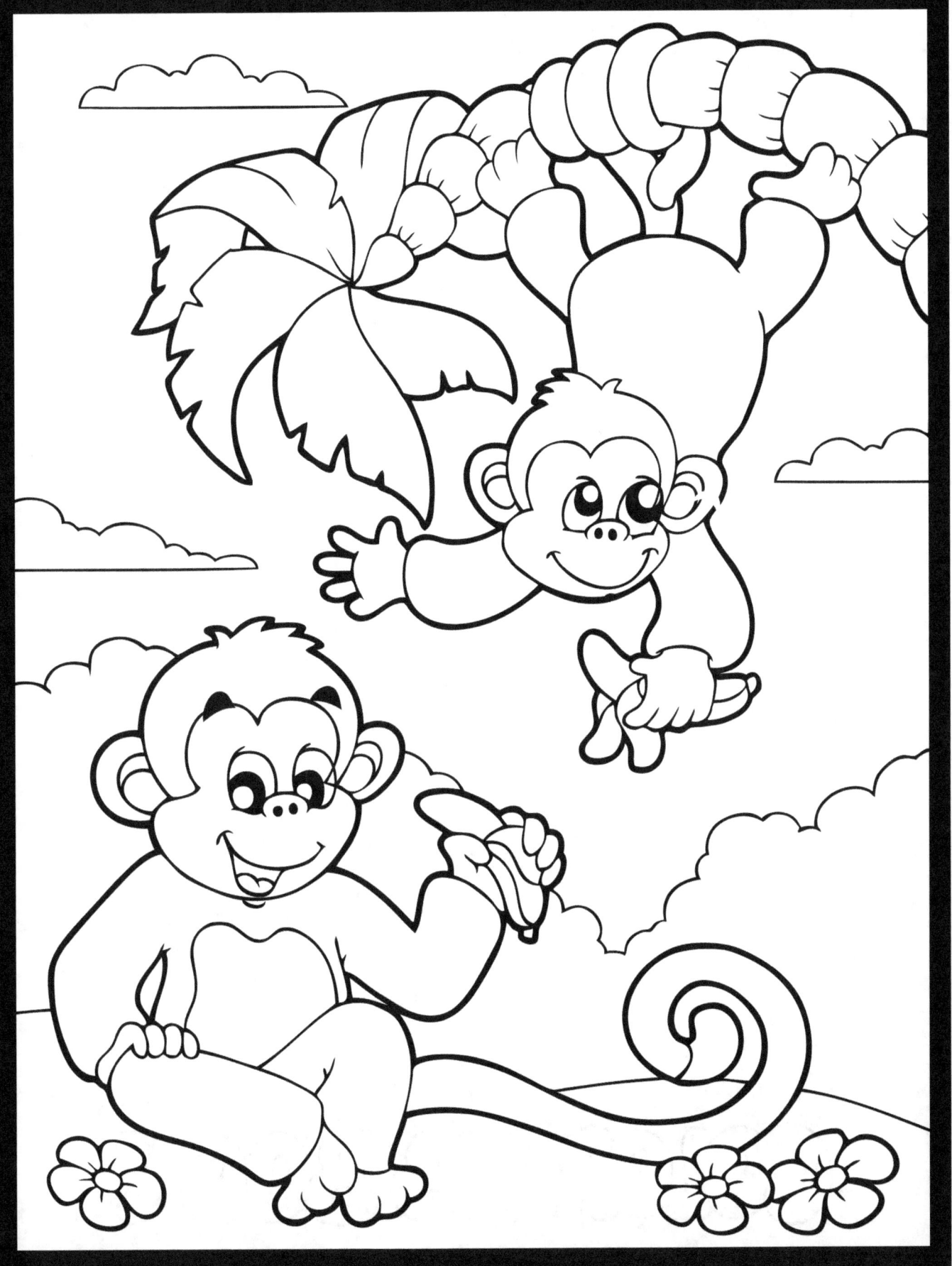

COLORING BOOK

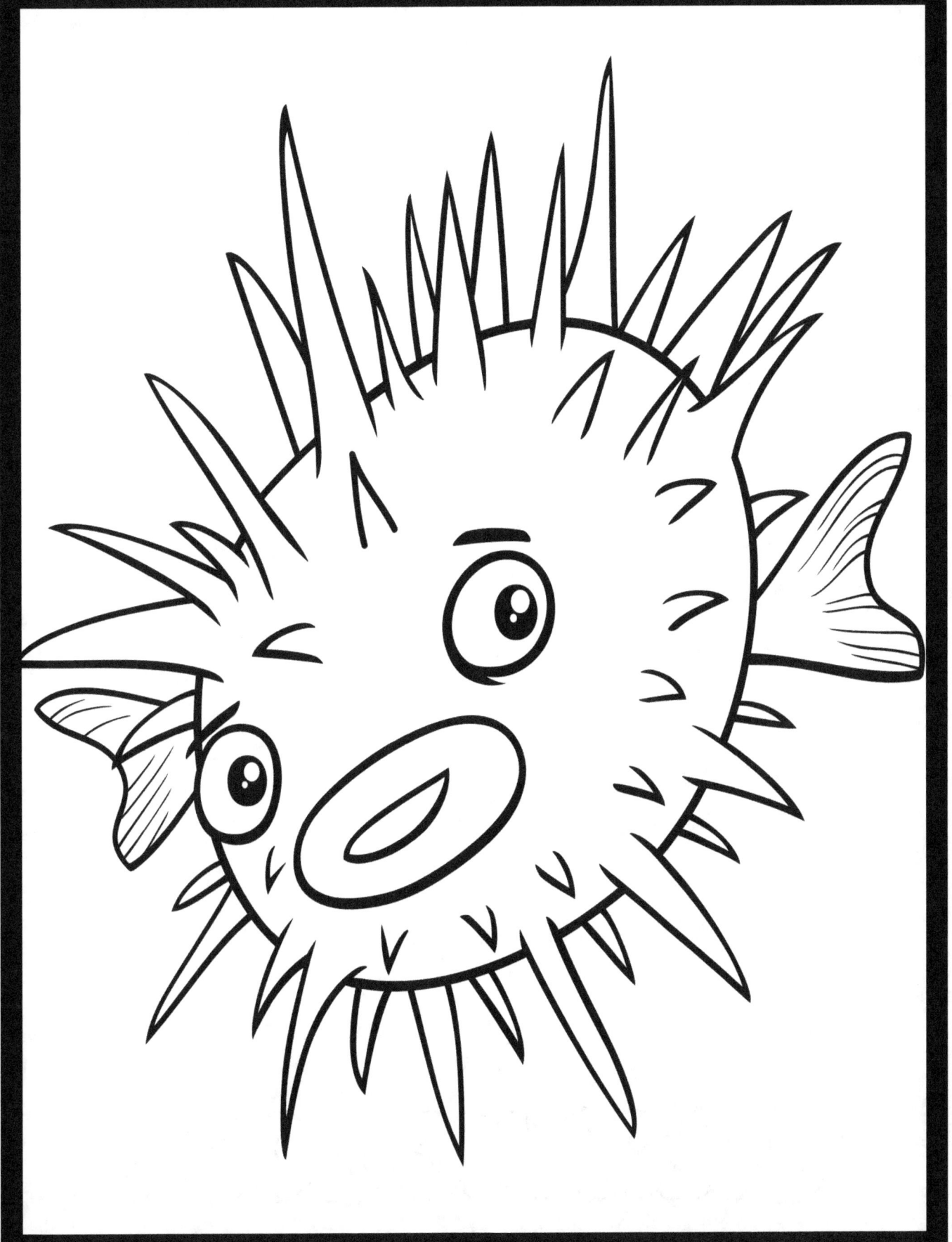

COLORING BOOK

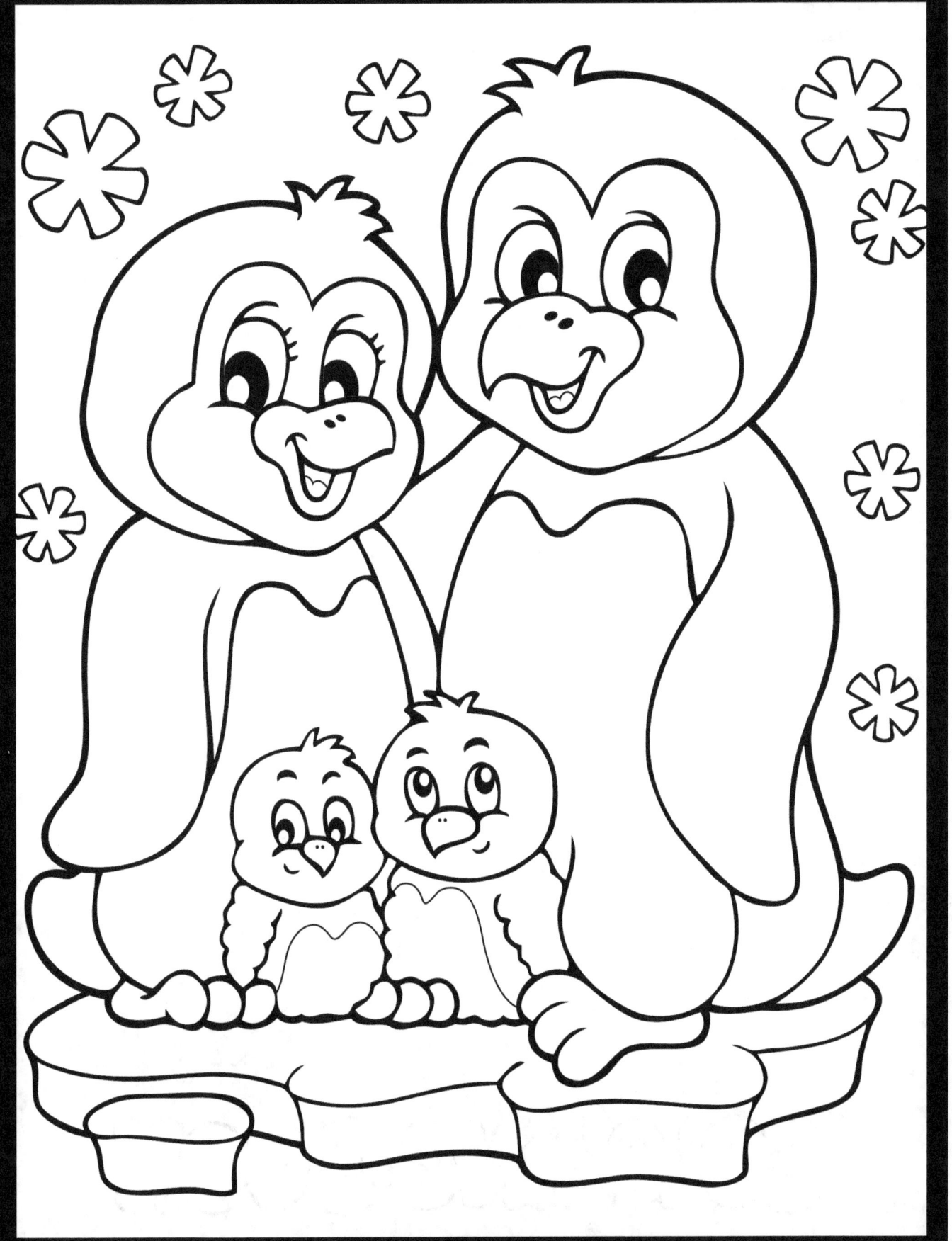

COLORING BOOK

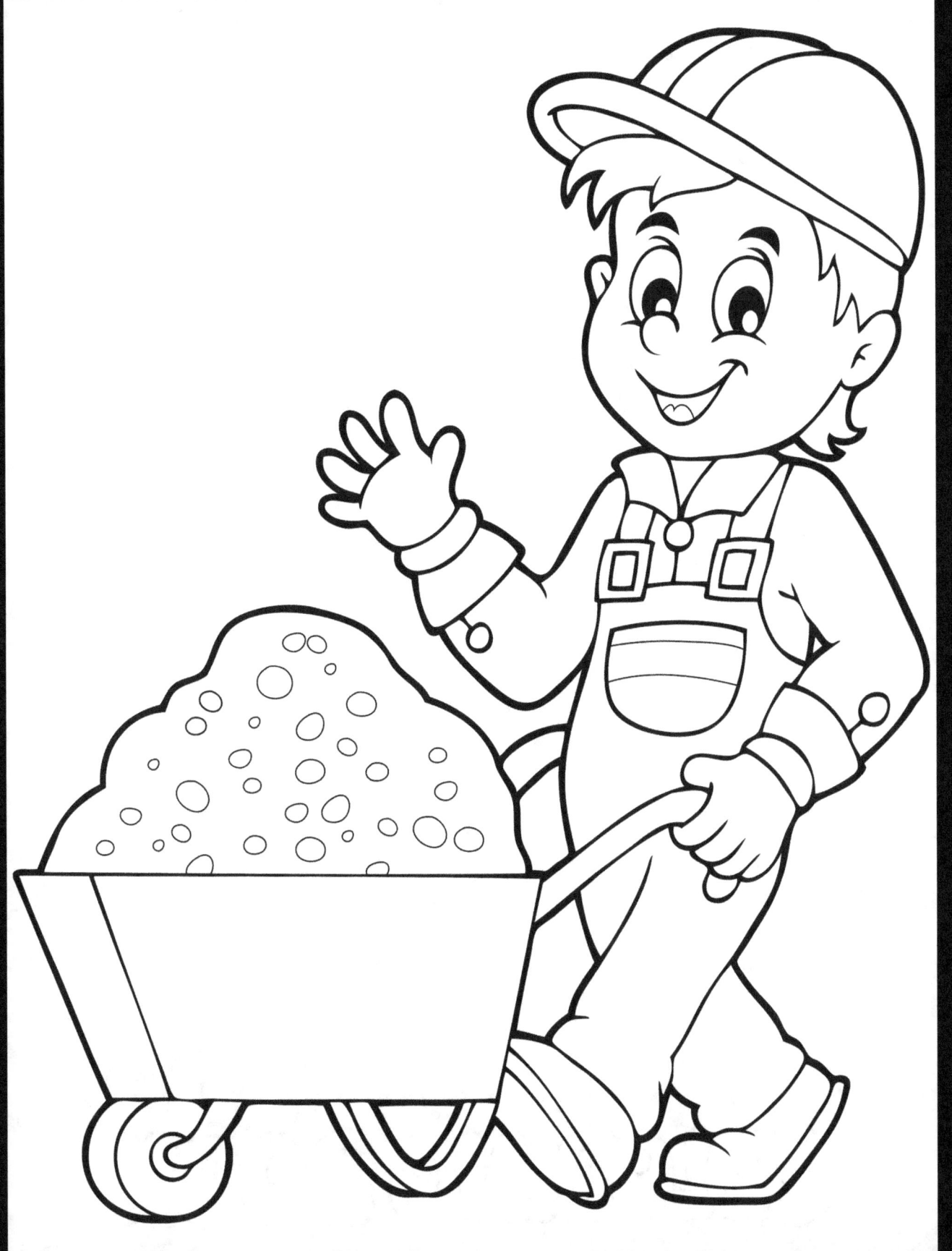

COLORING BOOK

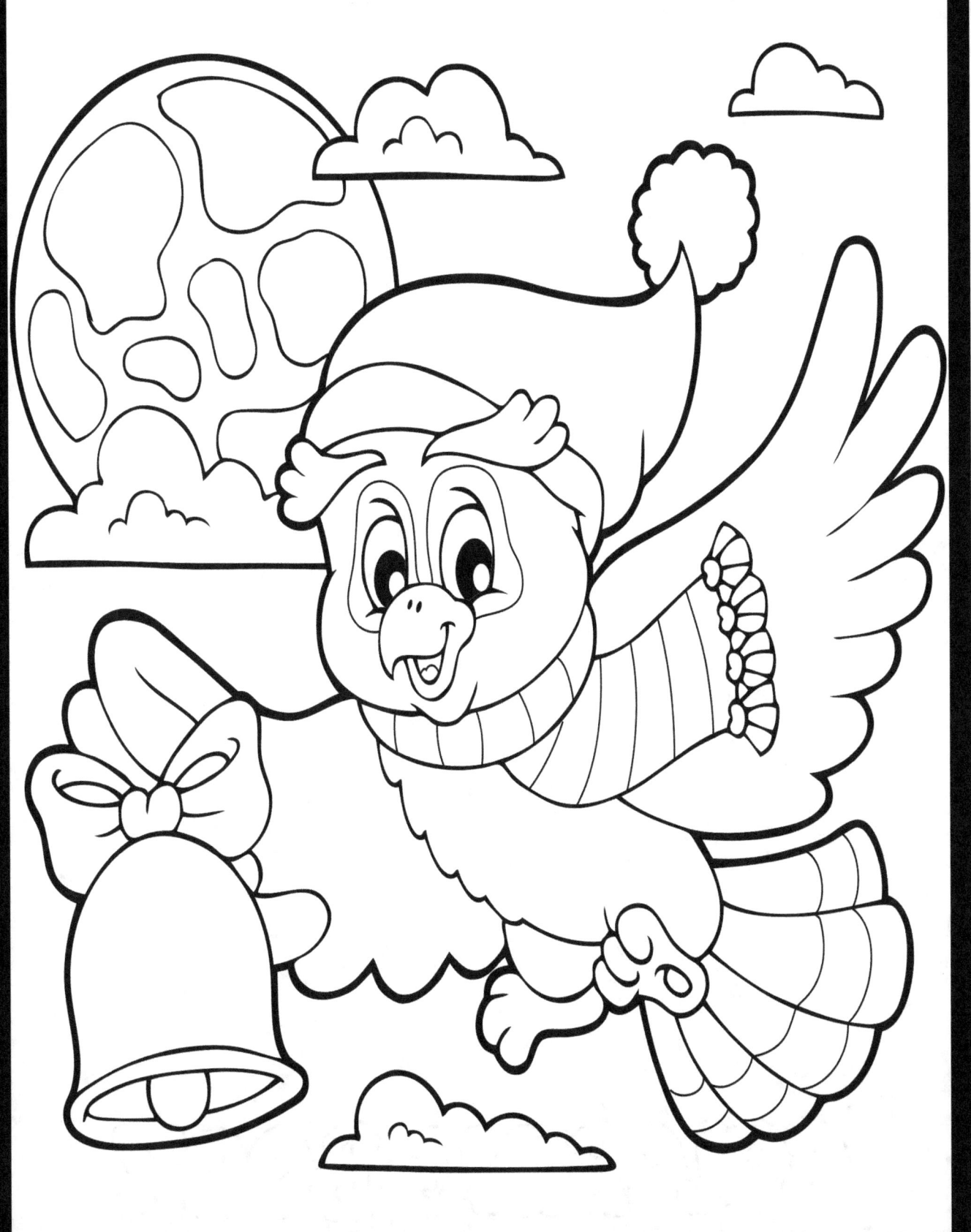

COLORING BOOK

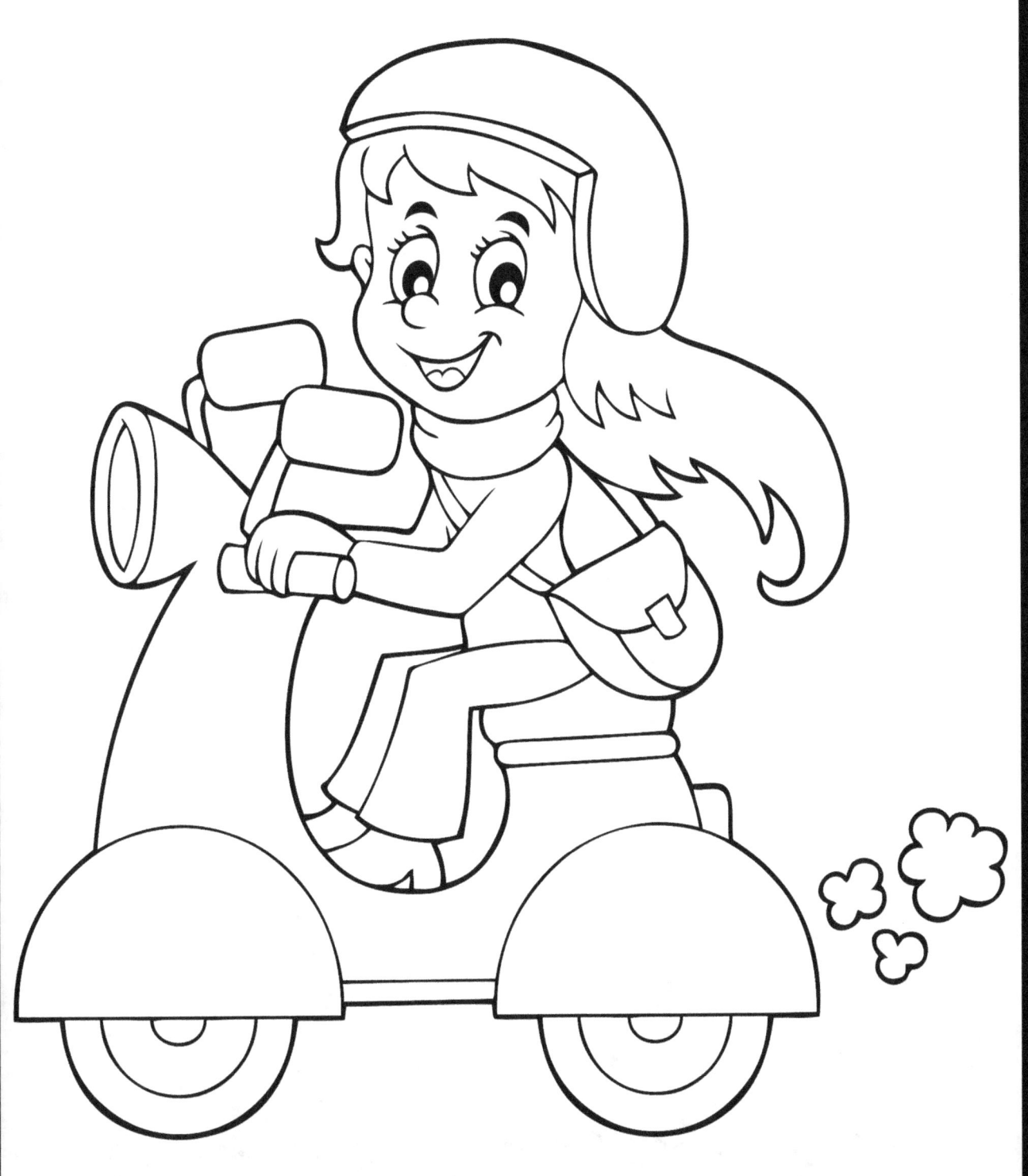

COLORING BOOK

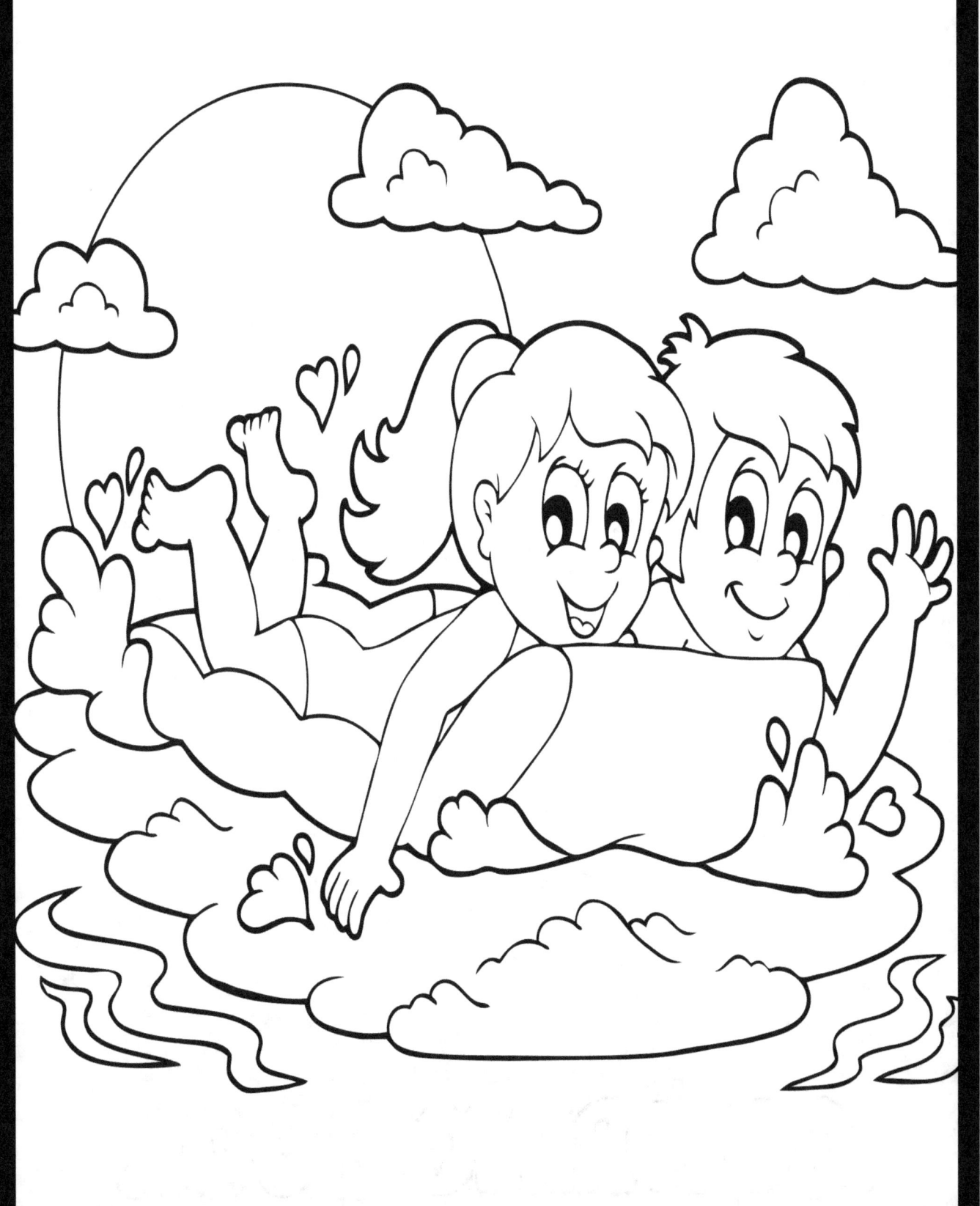

COLORING BOOK

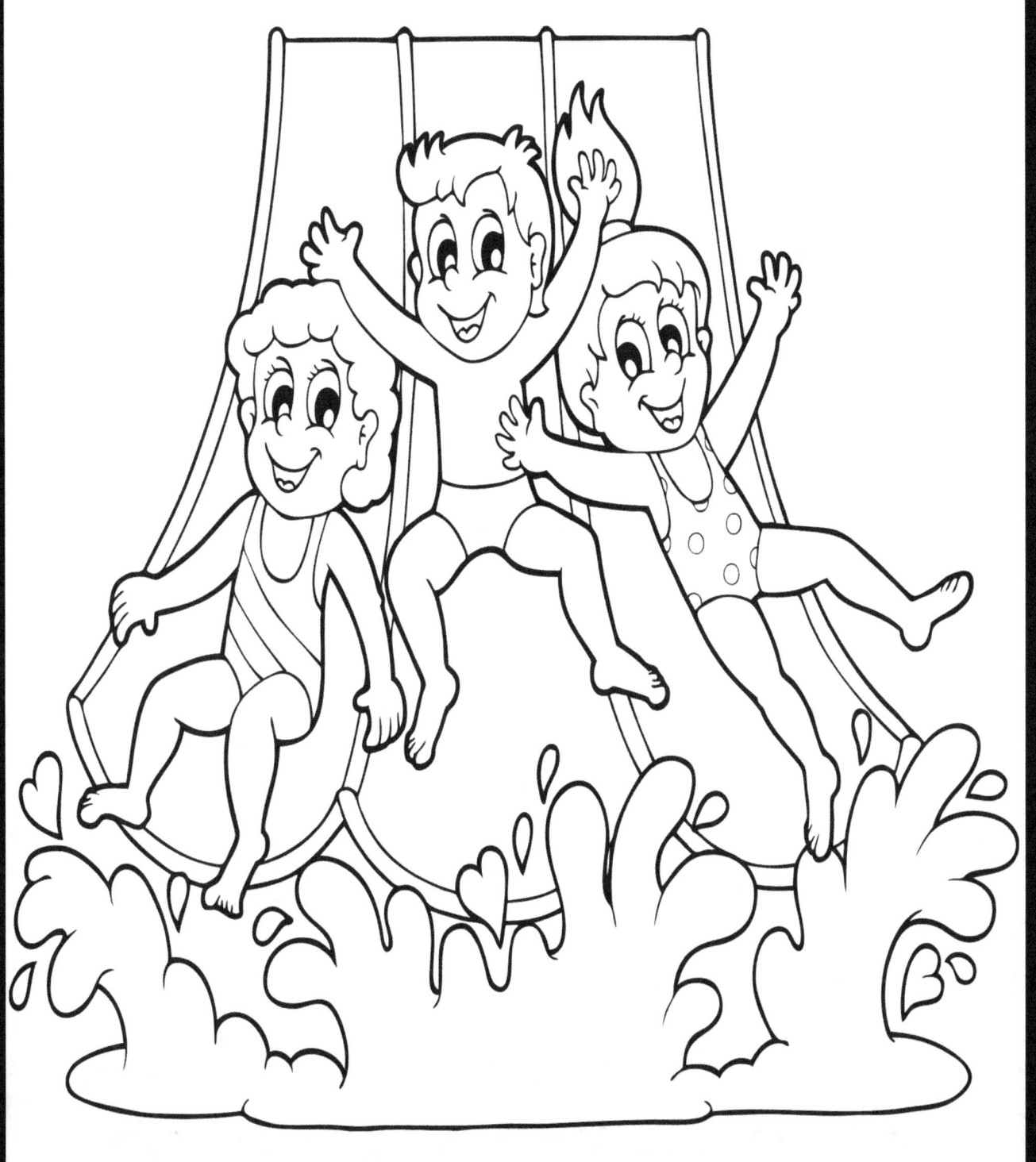

COLORING BOOK

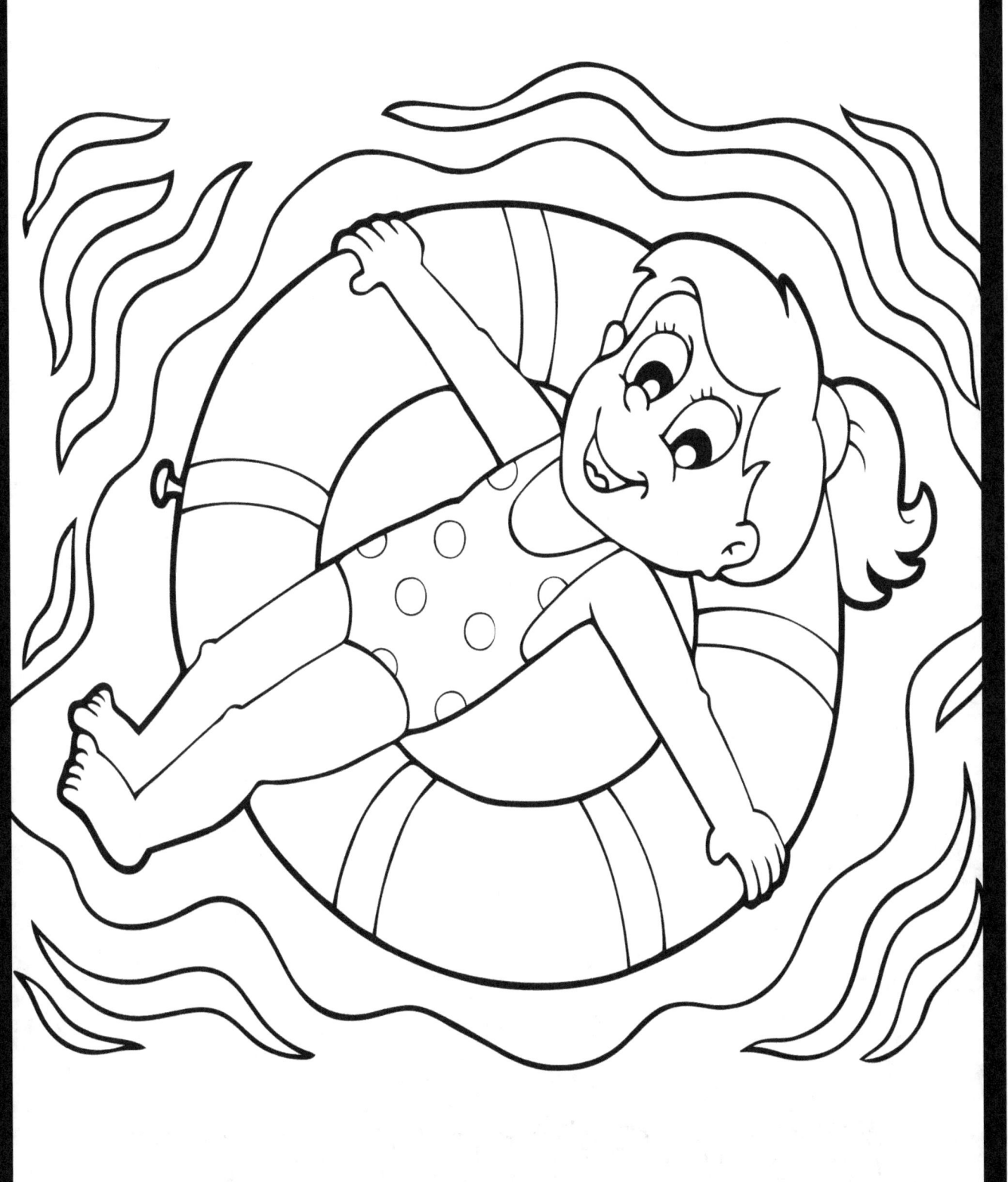

COLORING BOOK

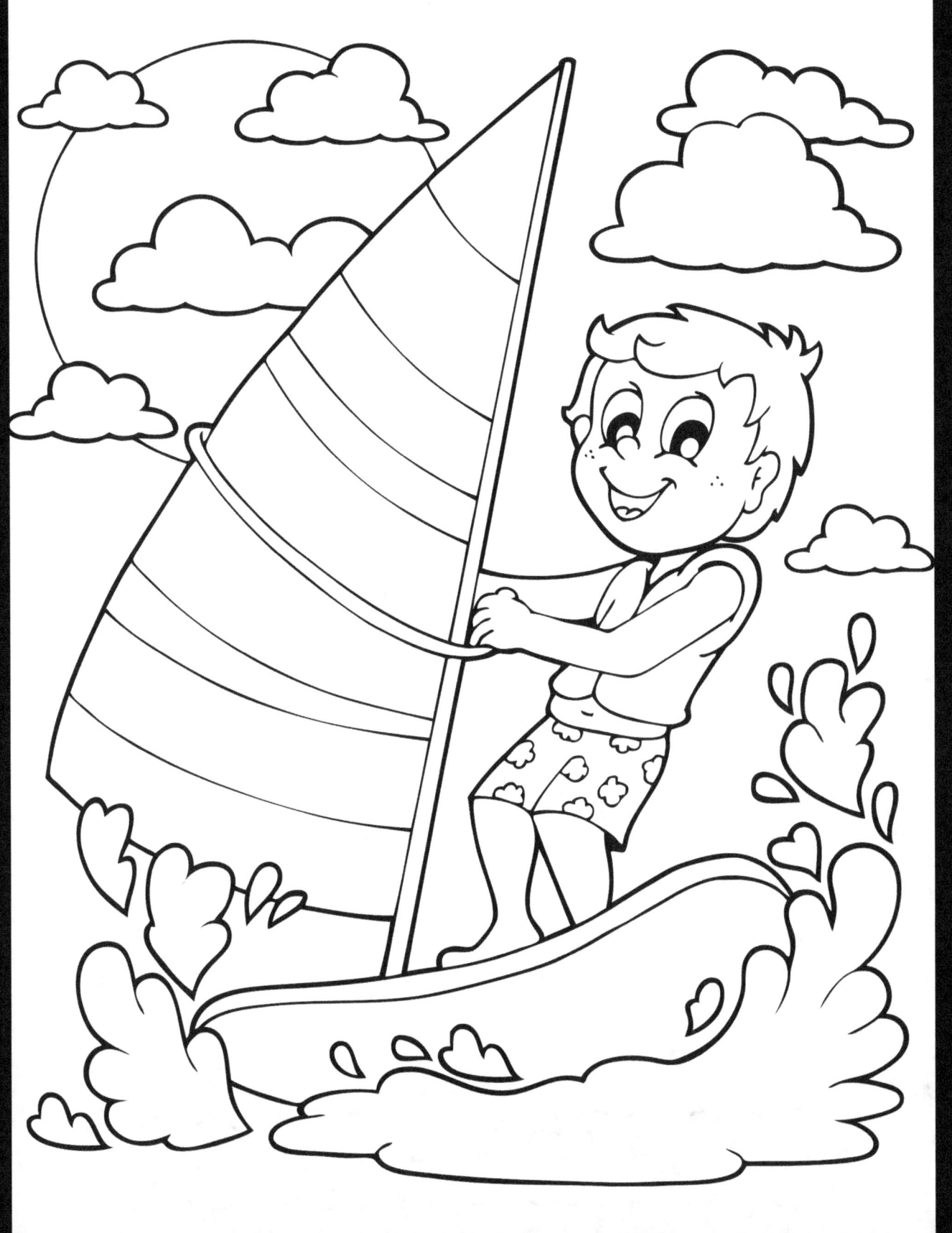

COLORING BOOK

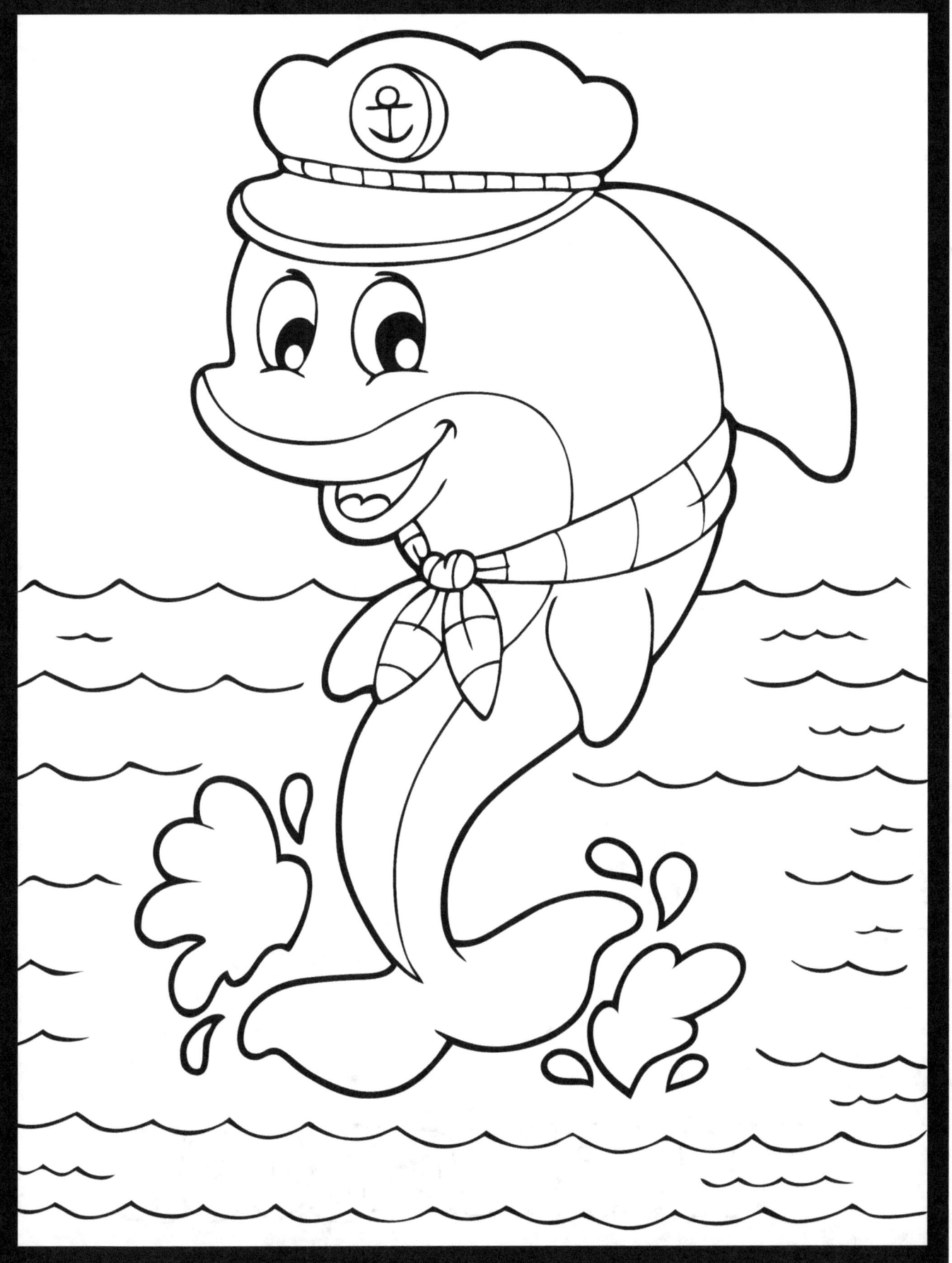

COLORING BOOK

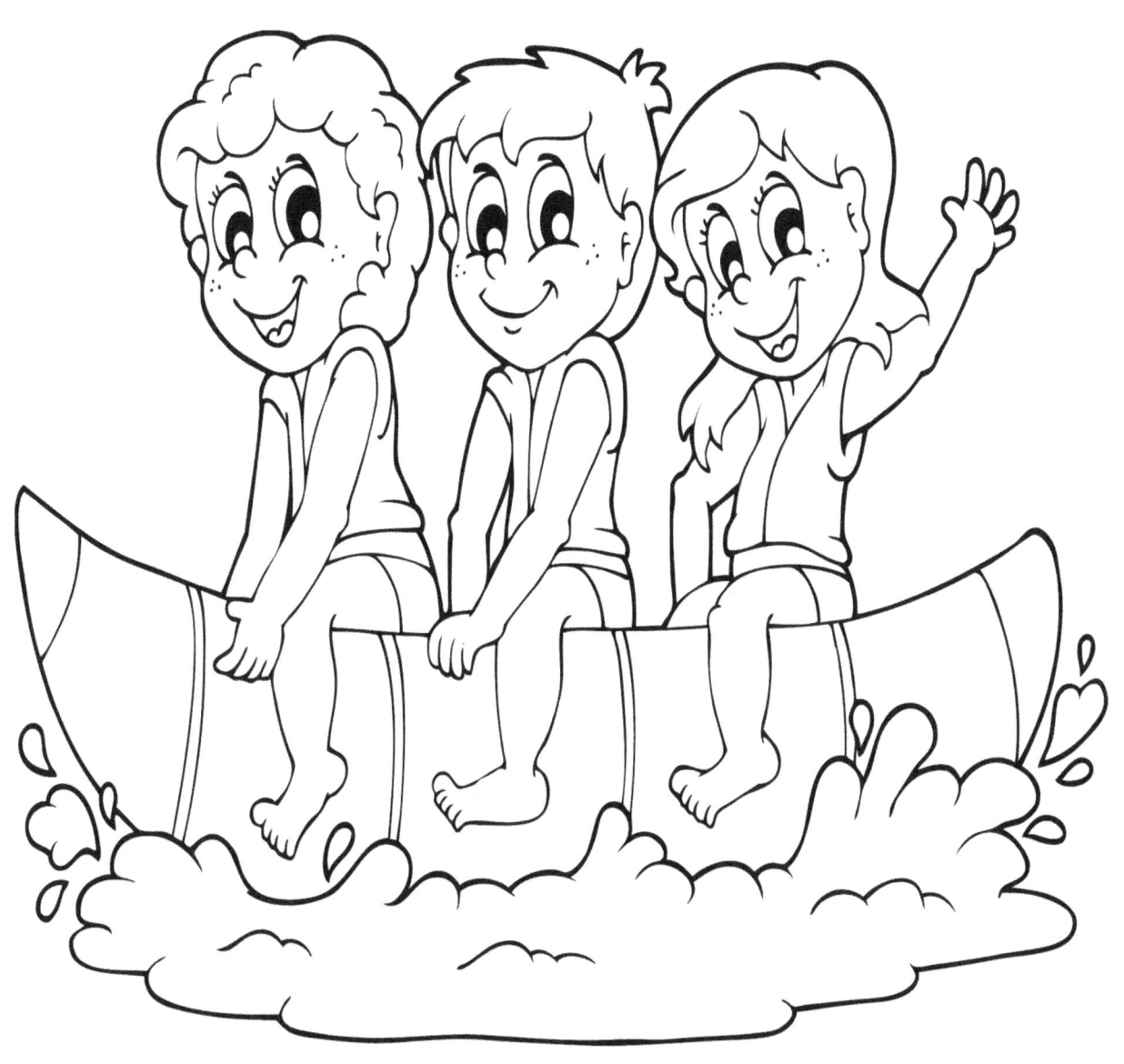

COLORING BOOK

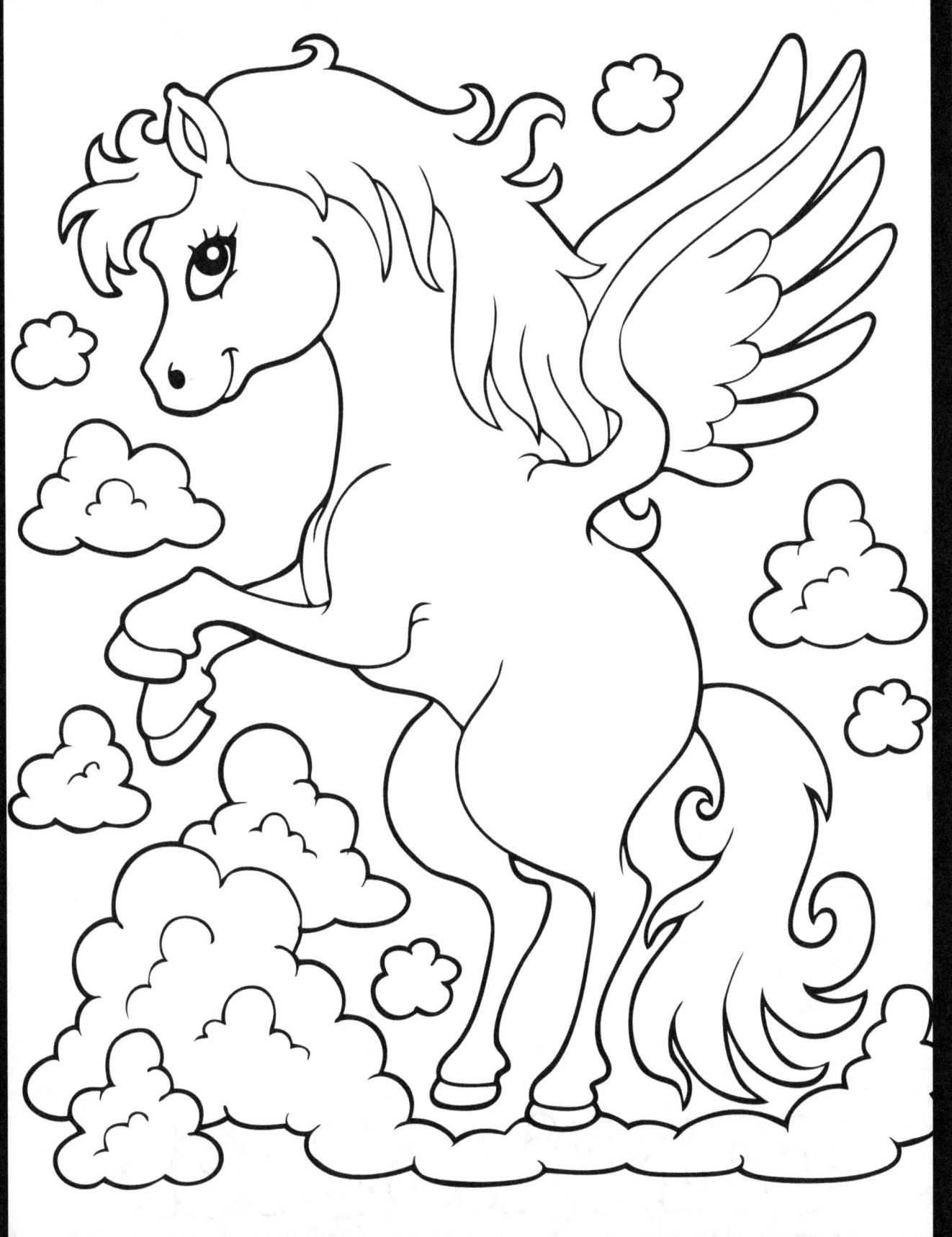

COLORING BOOK

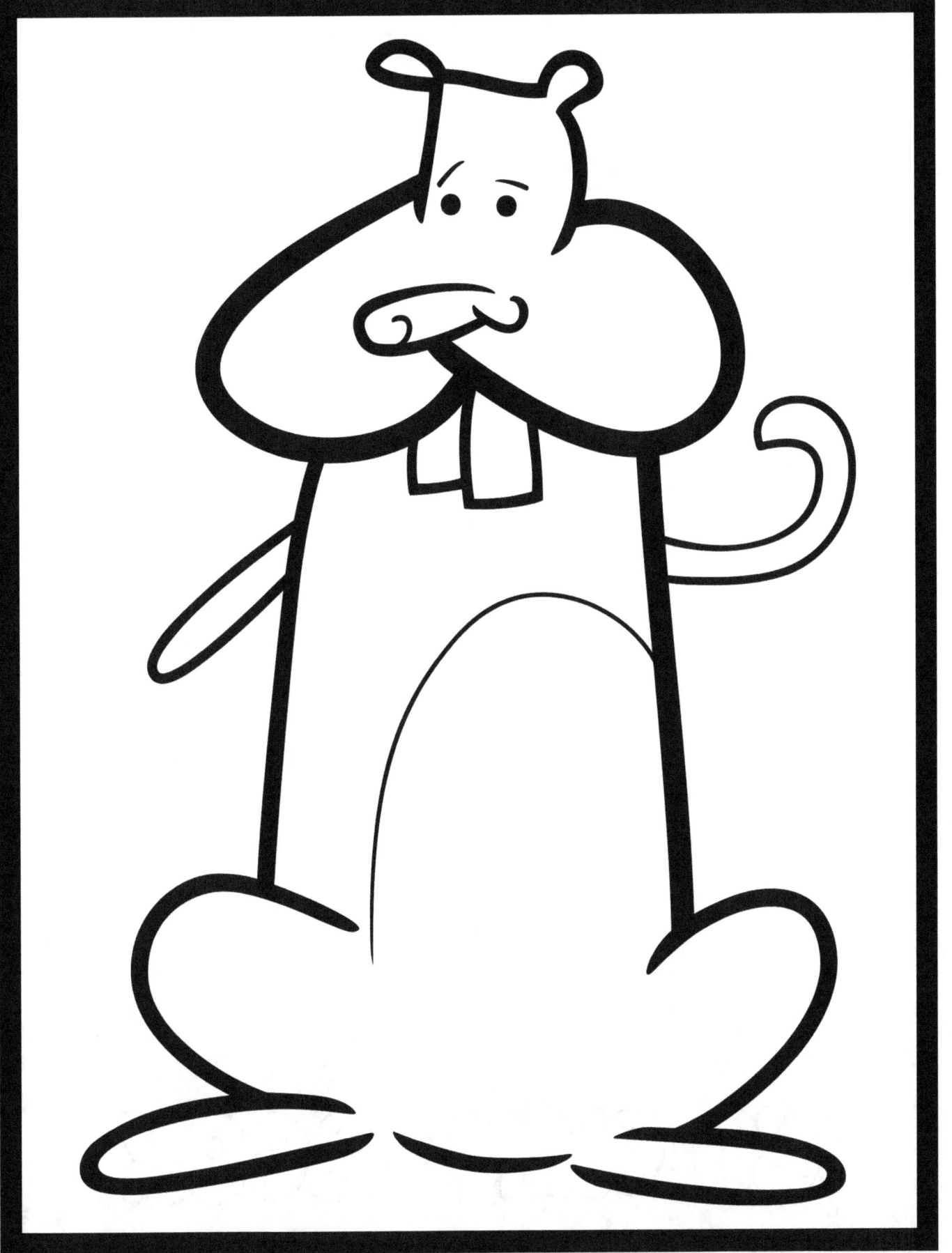

COLORING BOOK

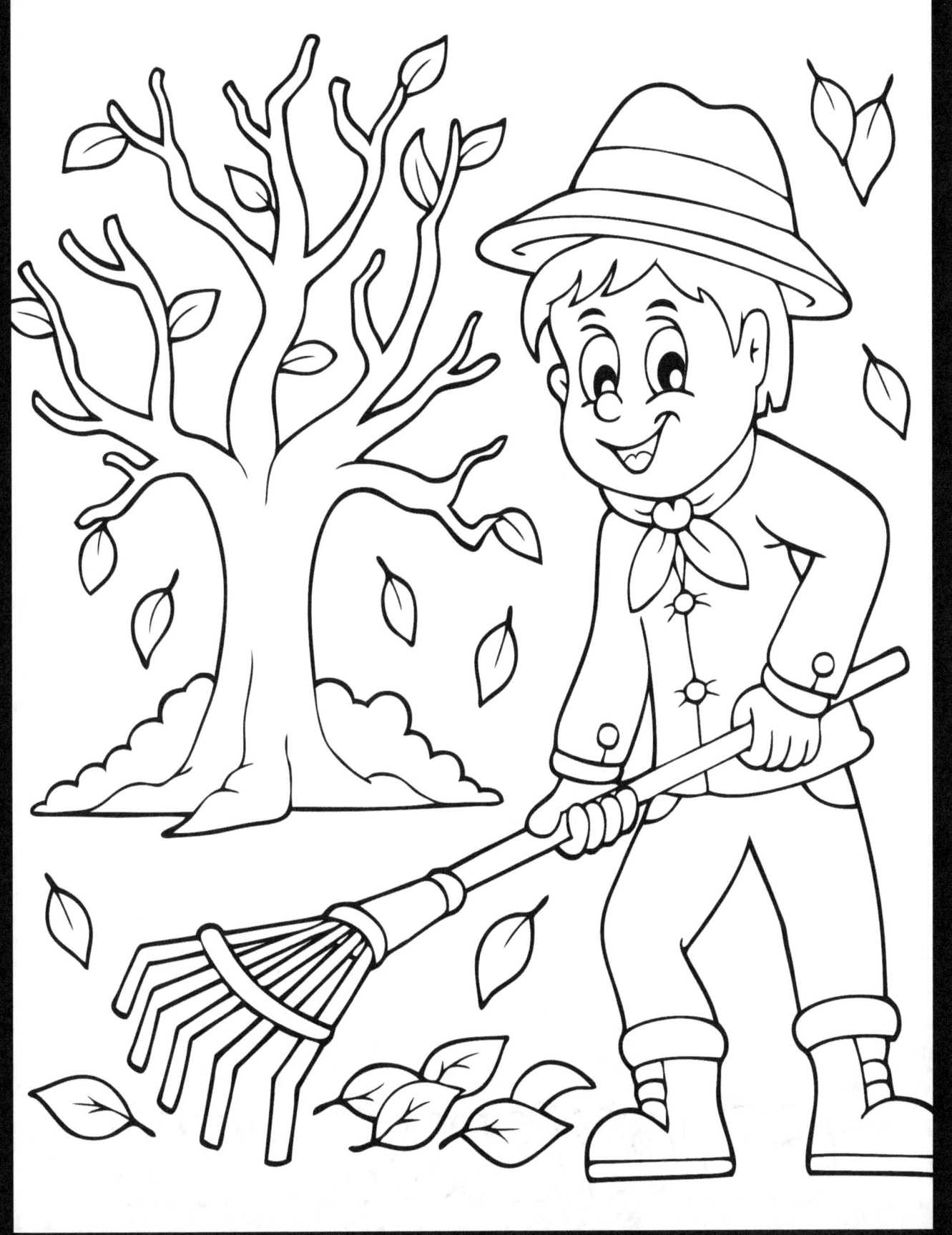

COLORING BOOK

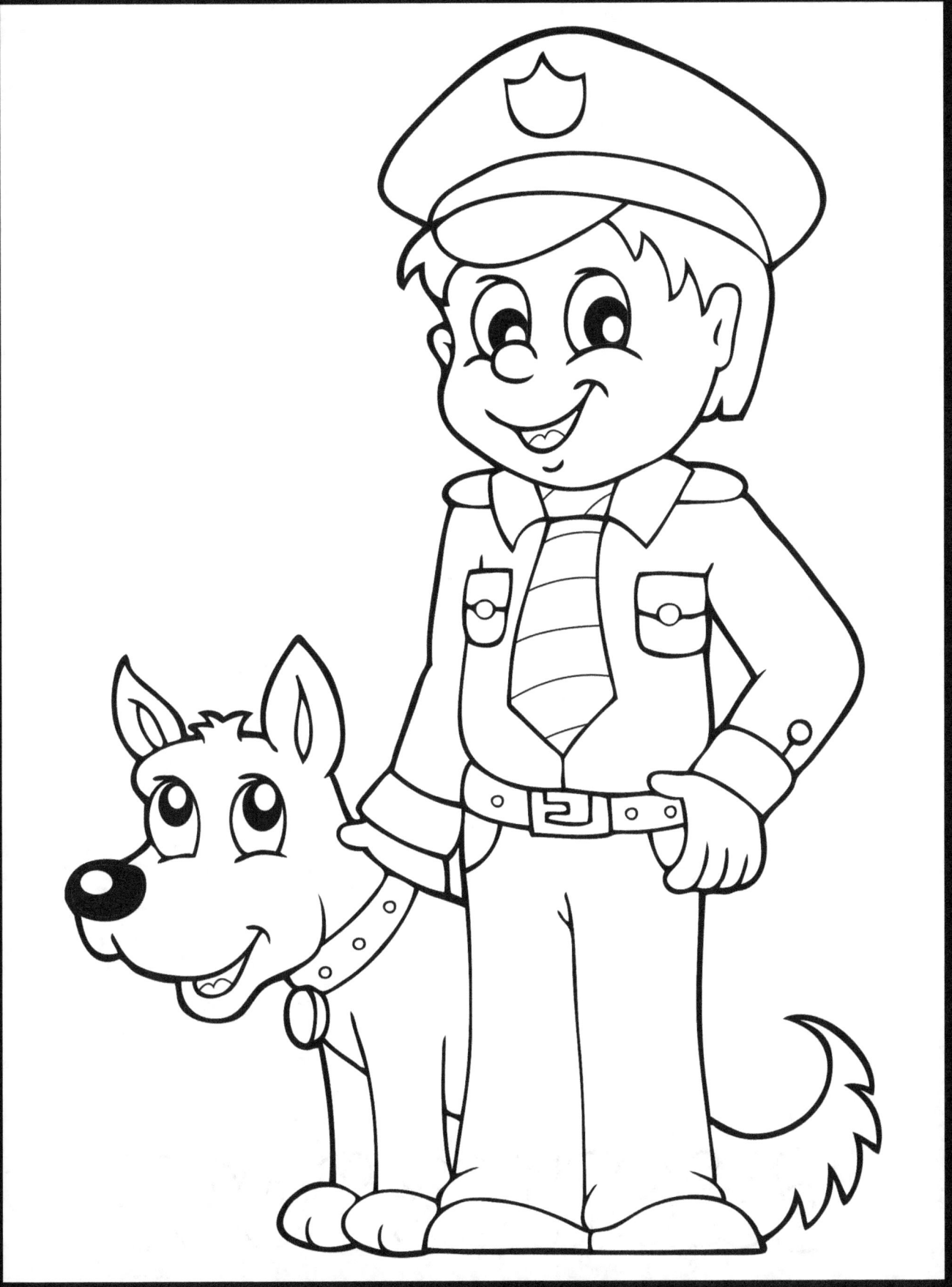

COLORING BOOK

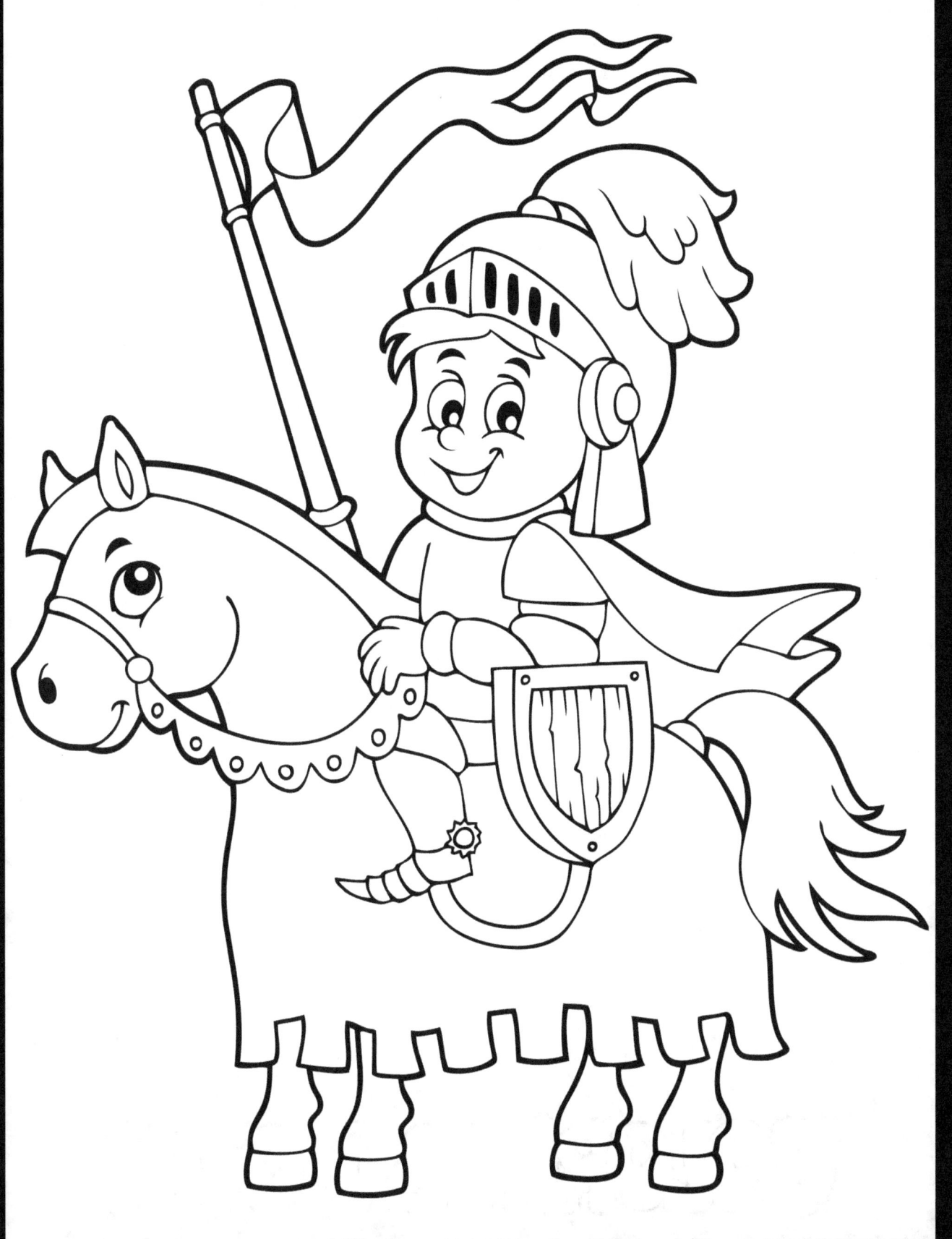

COLORING BOOK

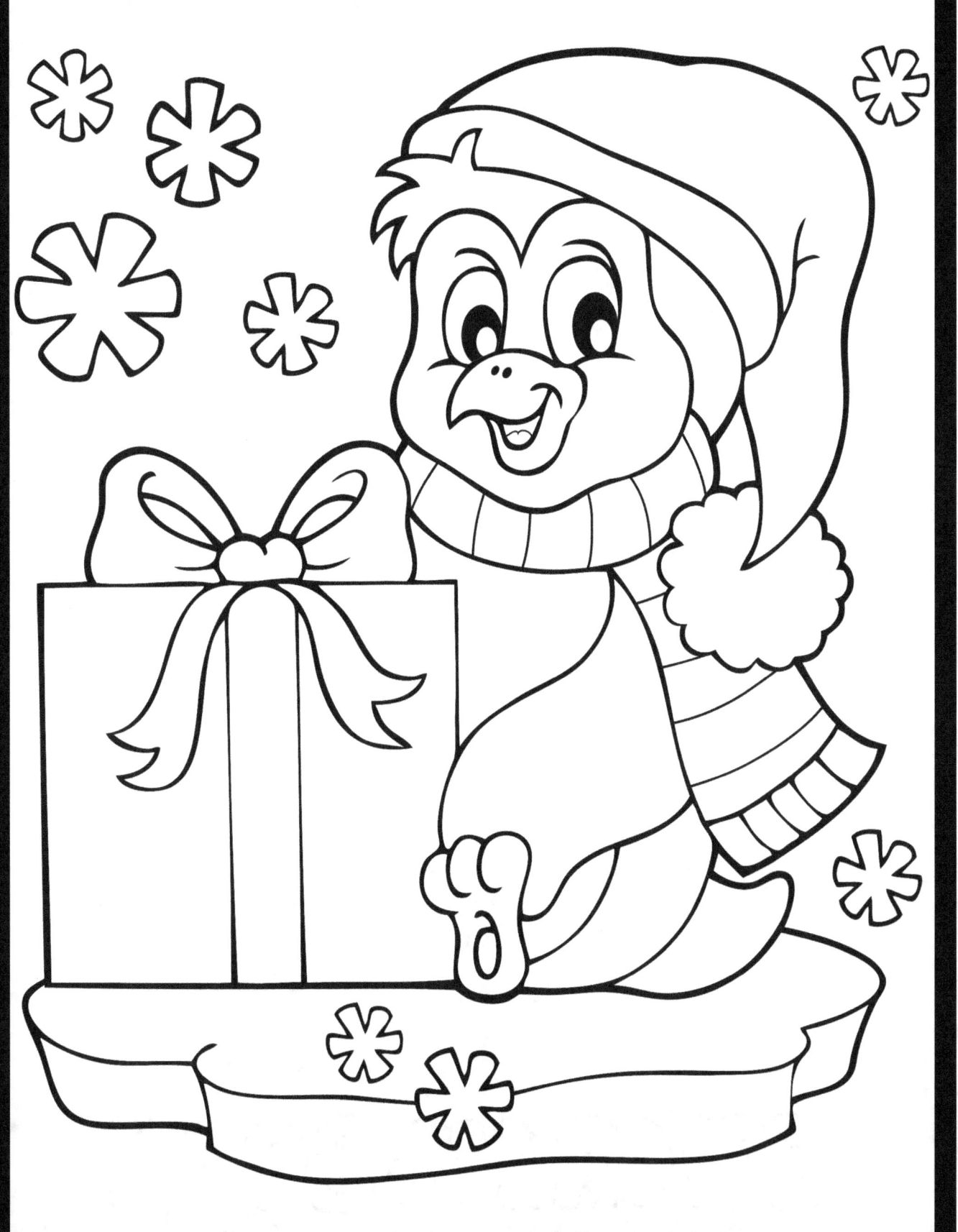

COLORING BOOK

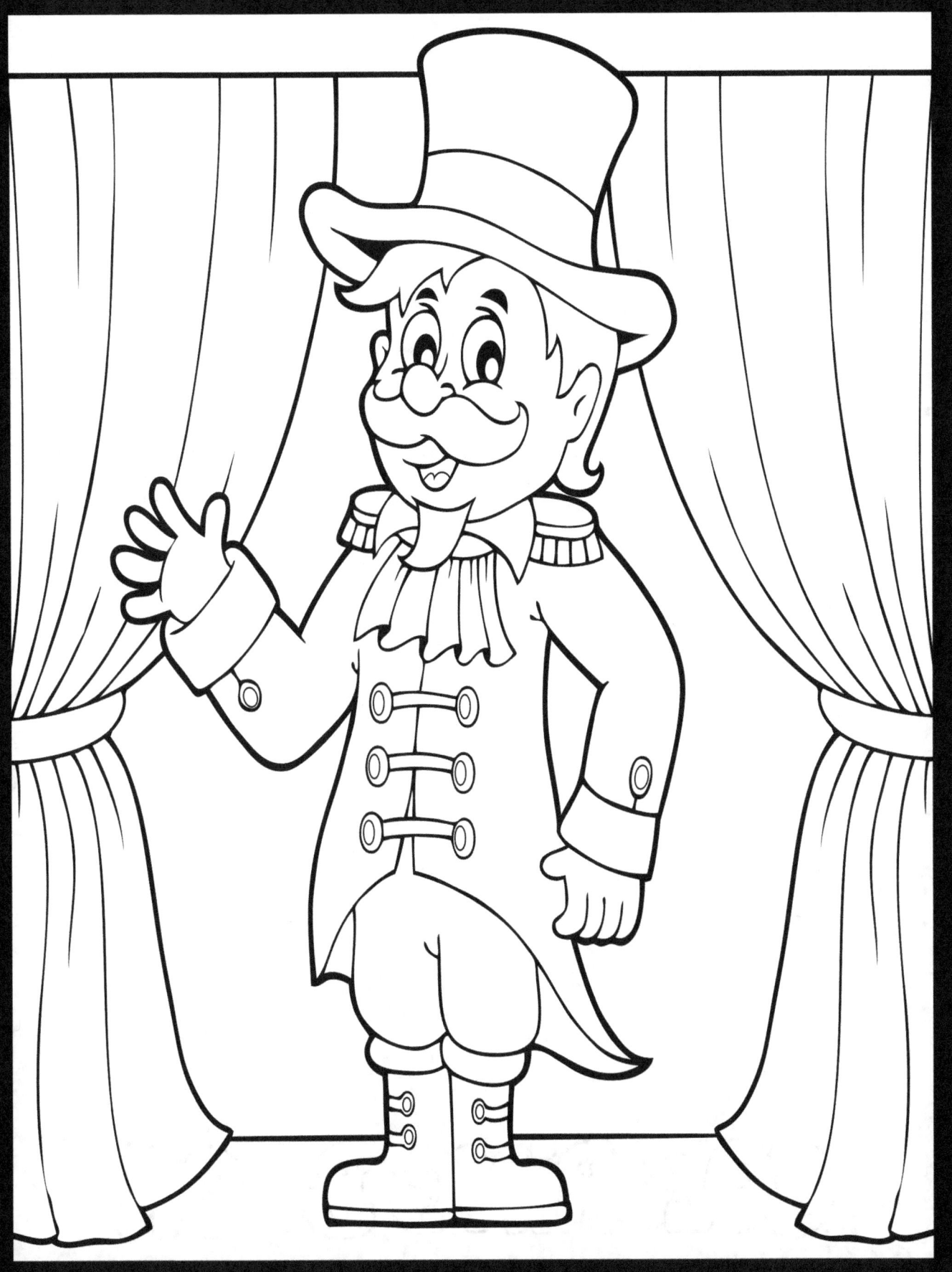

COLORING BOOK

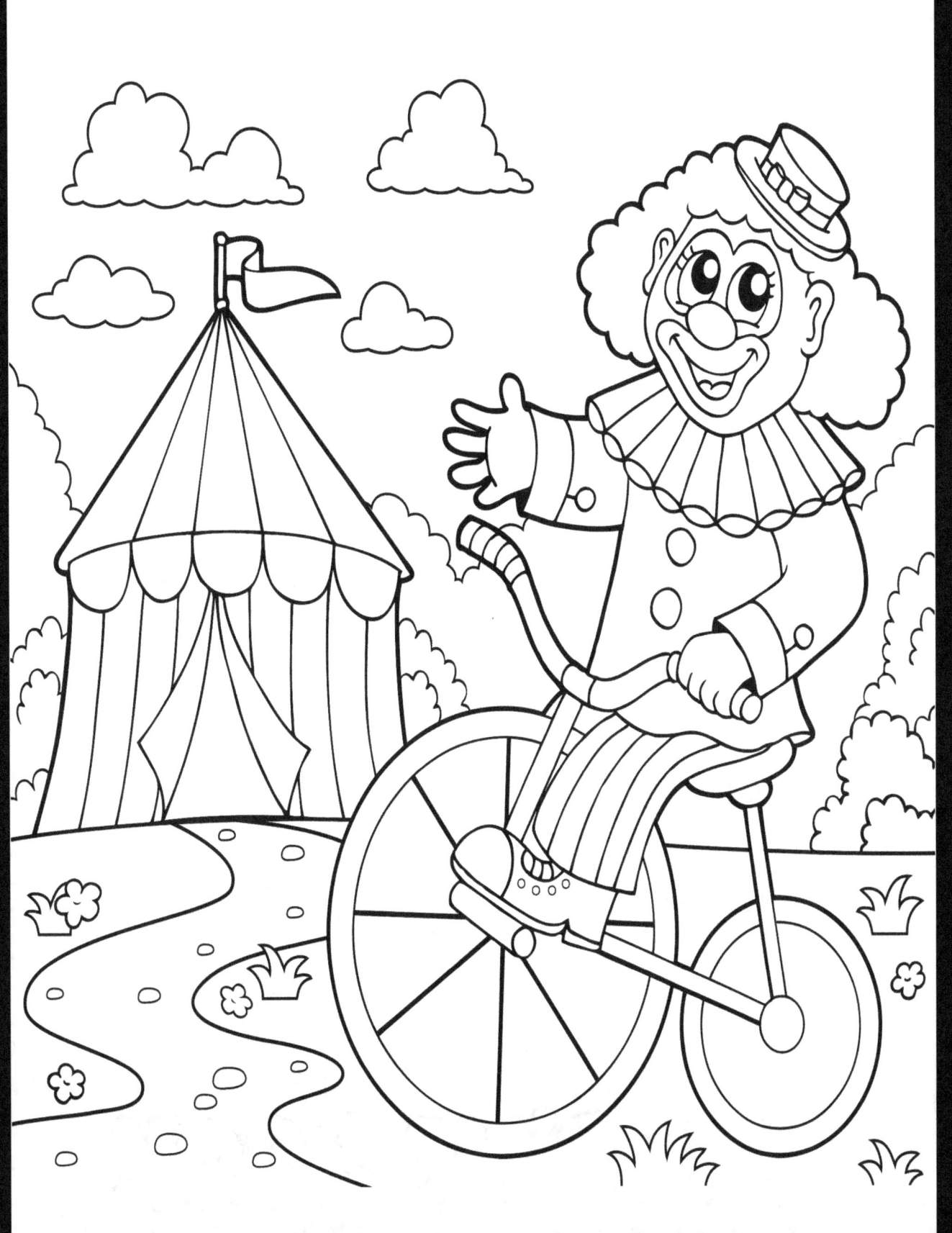

COLORiNG BOOK

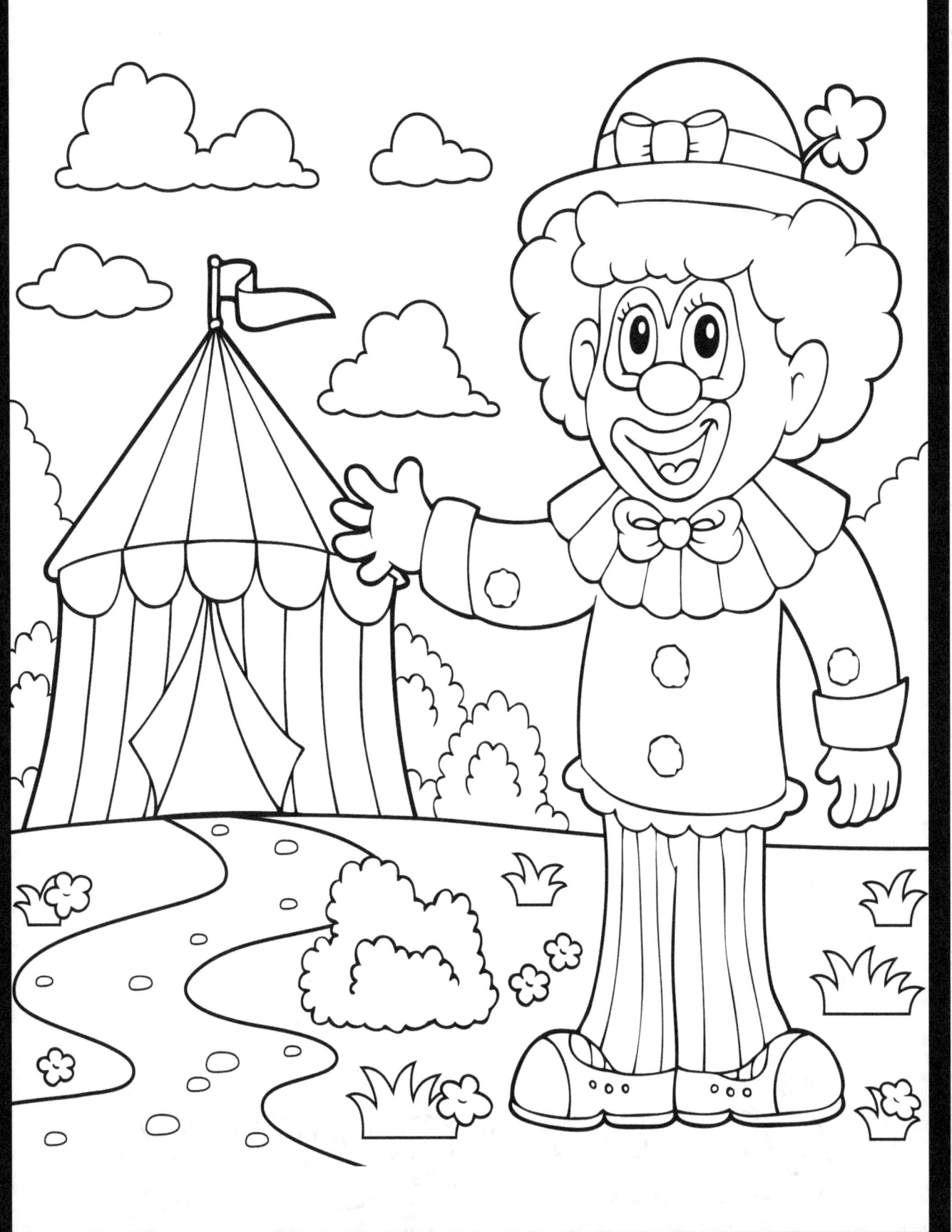

COLORING BOOK

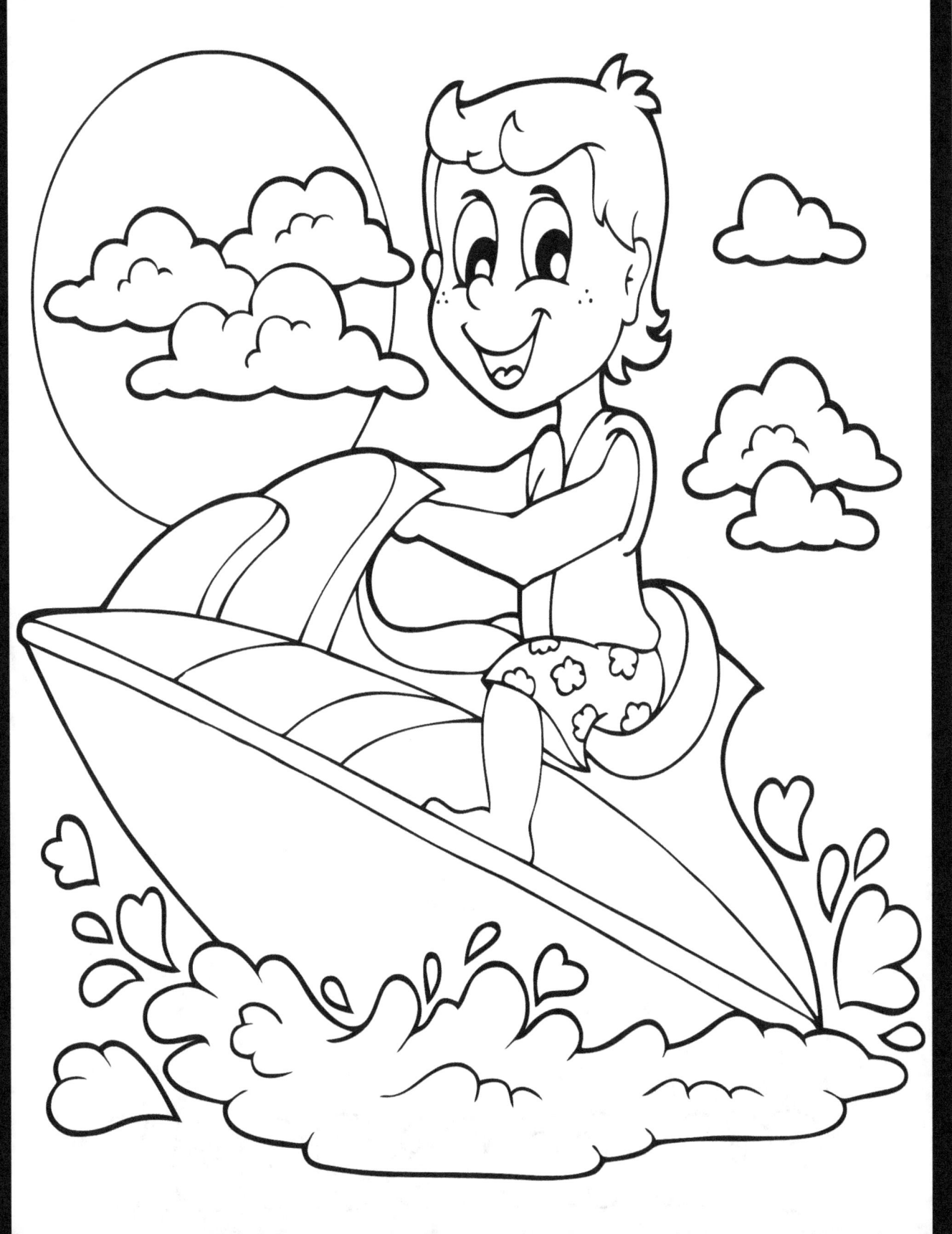

COLORING BOOK

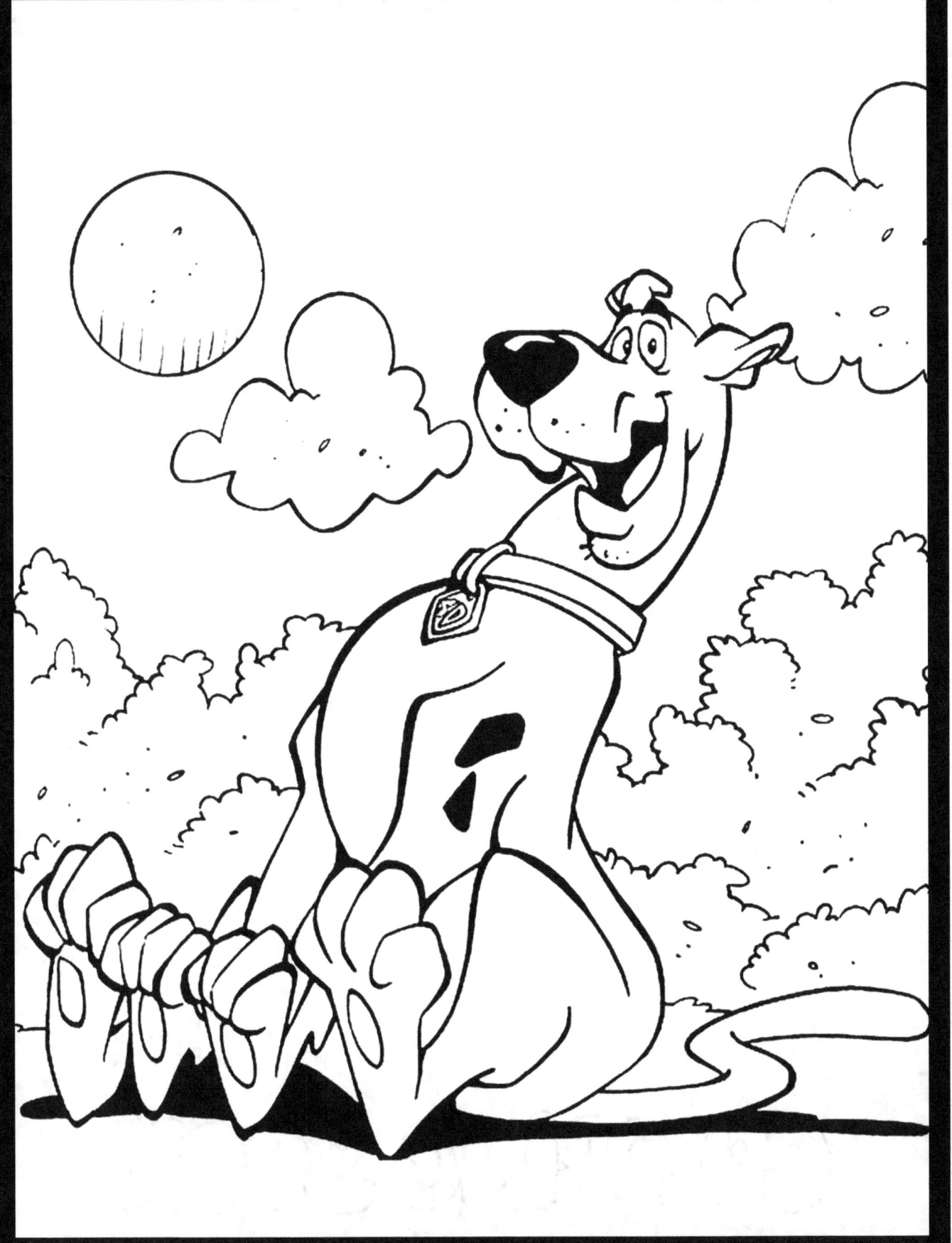

COLORING BOOK

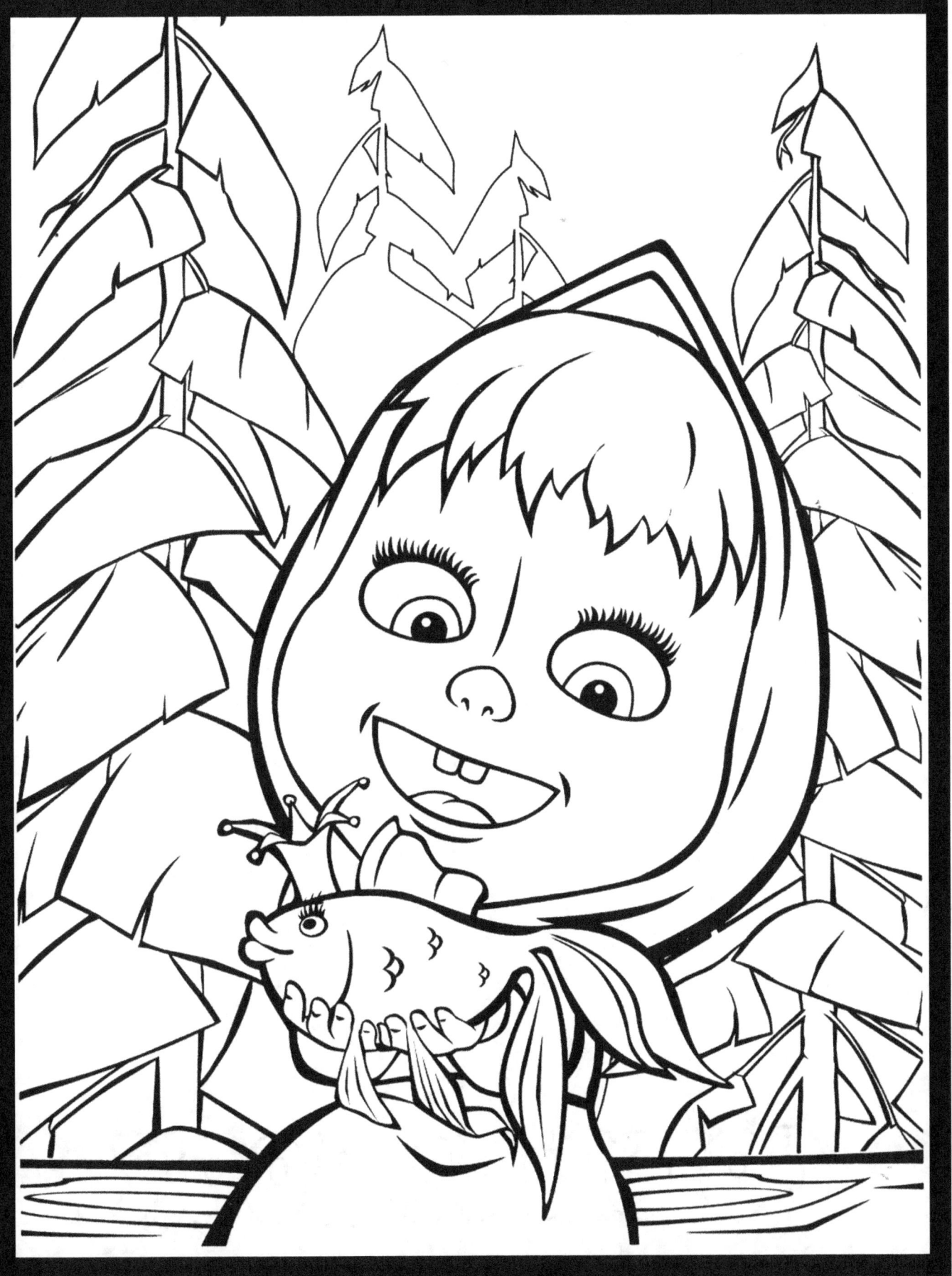

COLORING BOOK

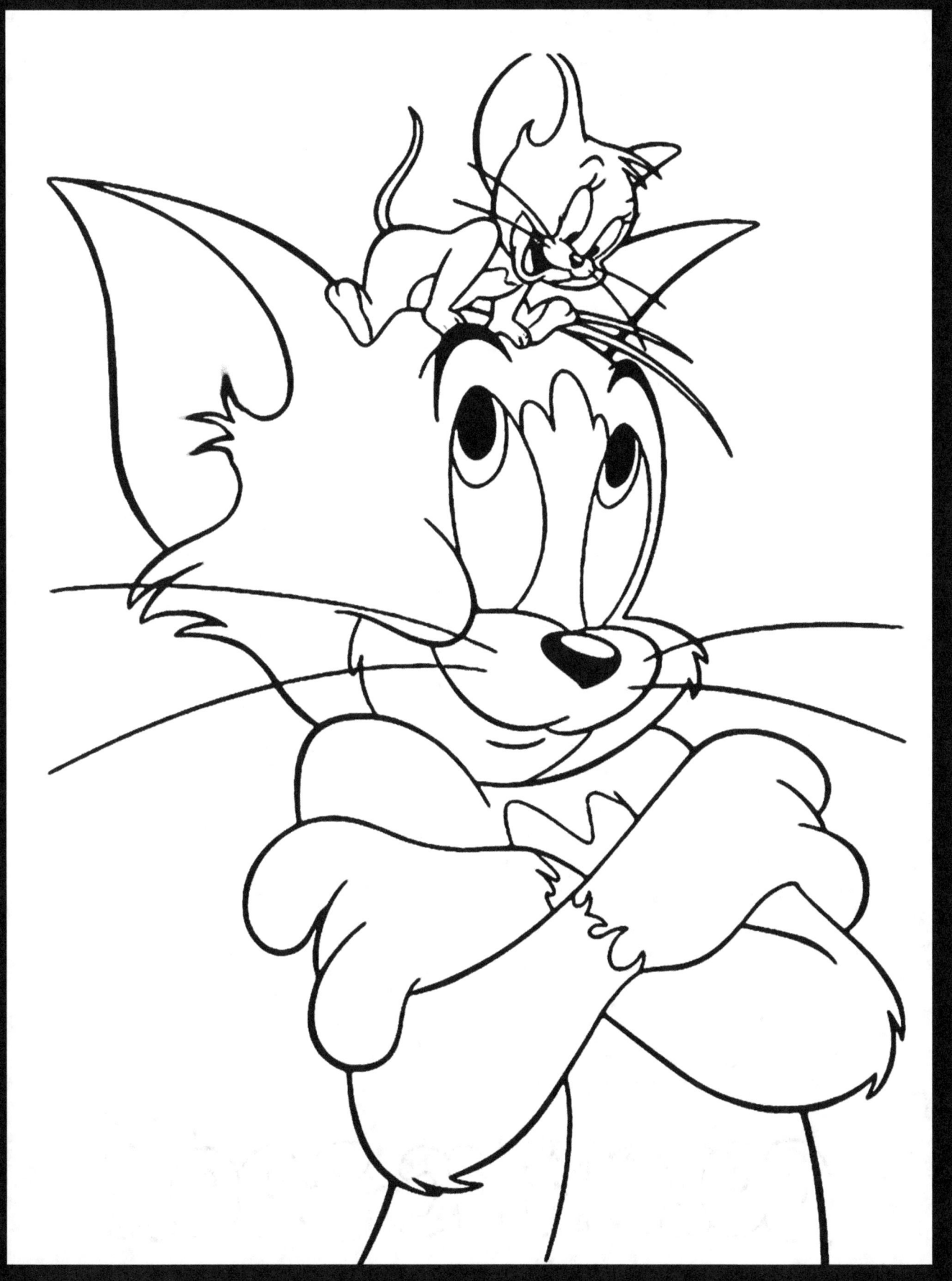

COLORING BOOK

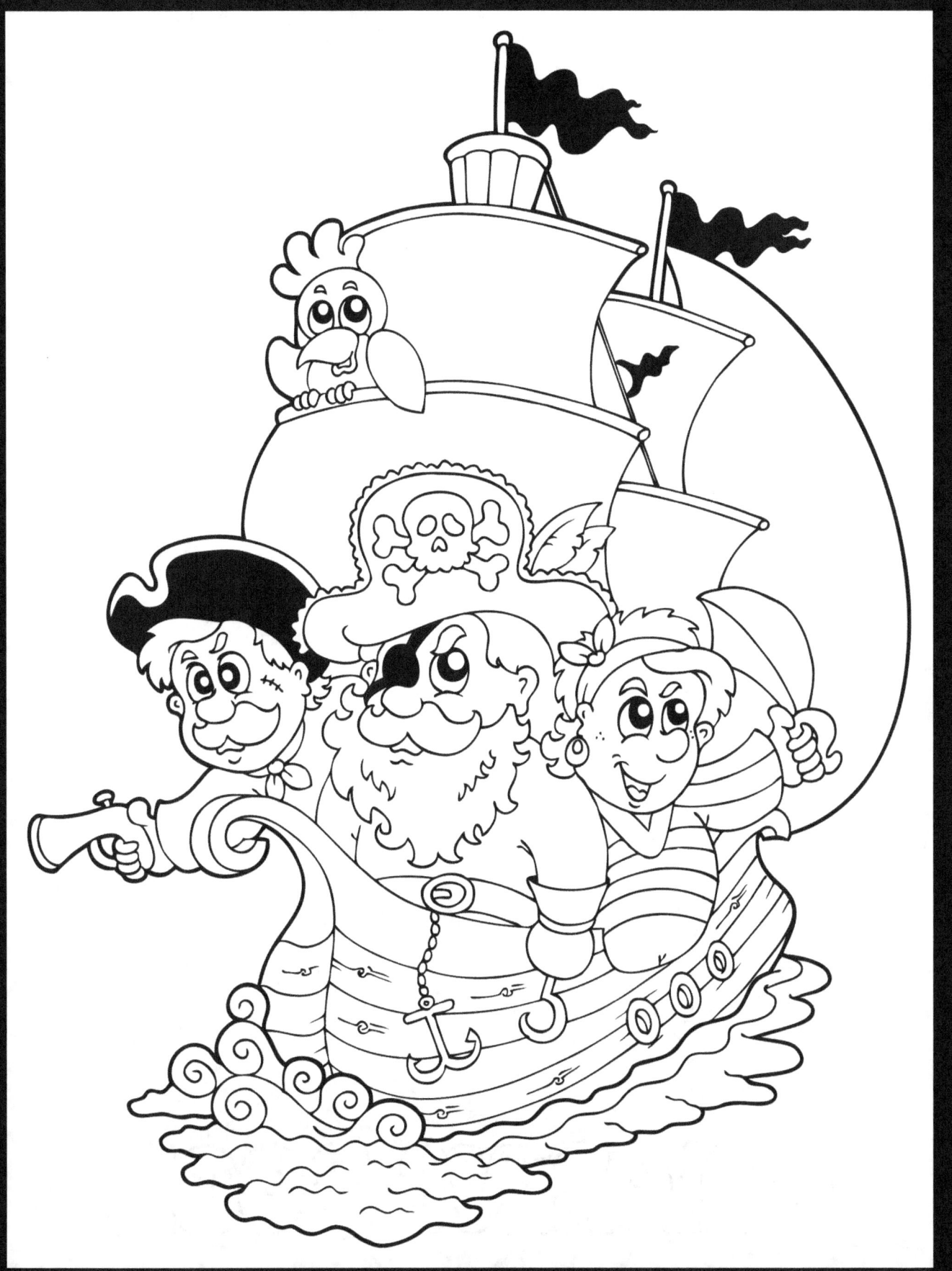

COLORING BOOK

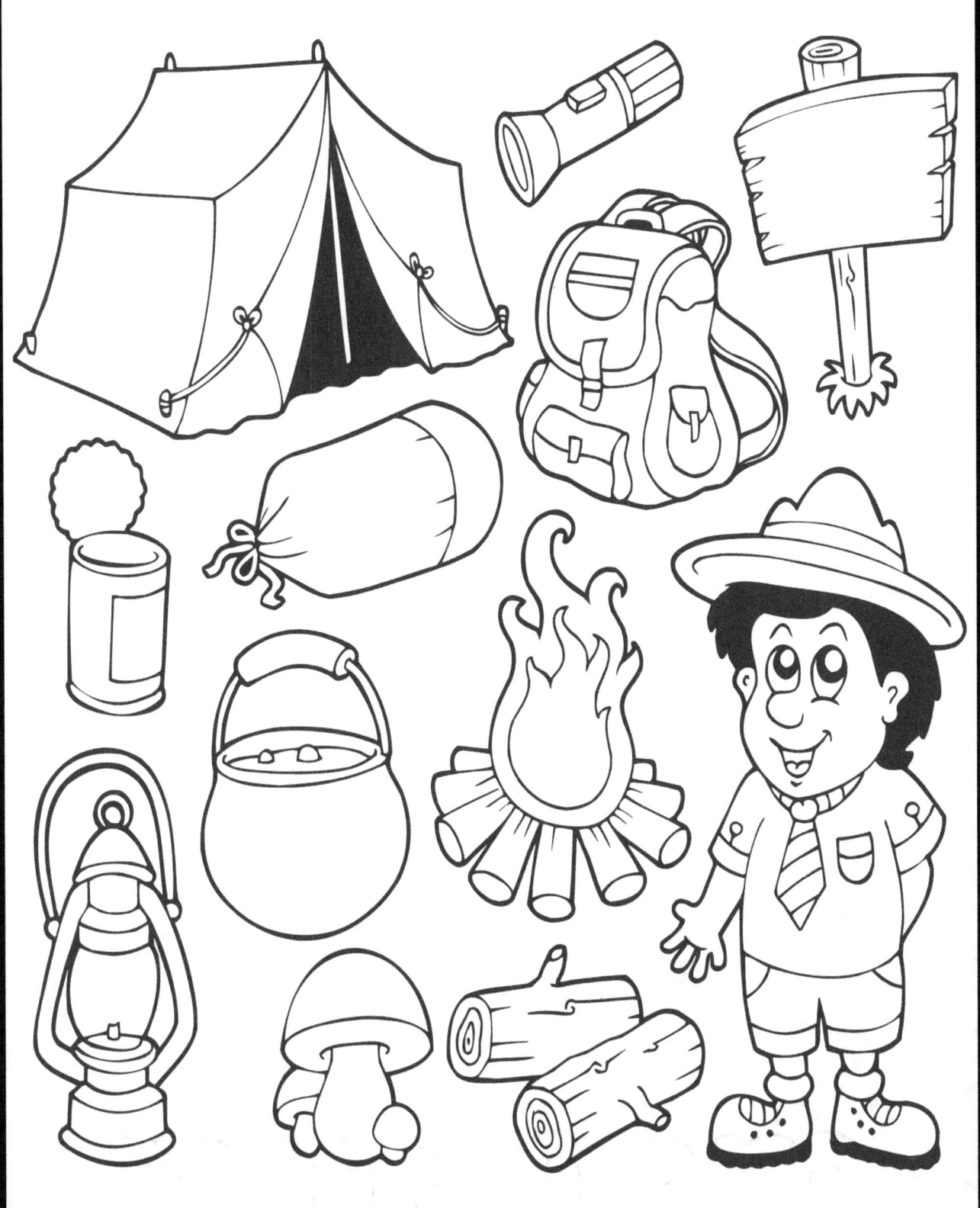

COLORING BOOK

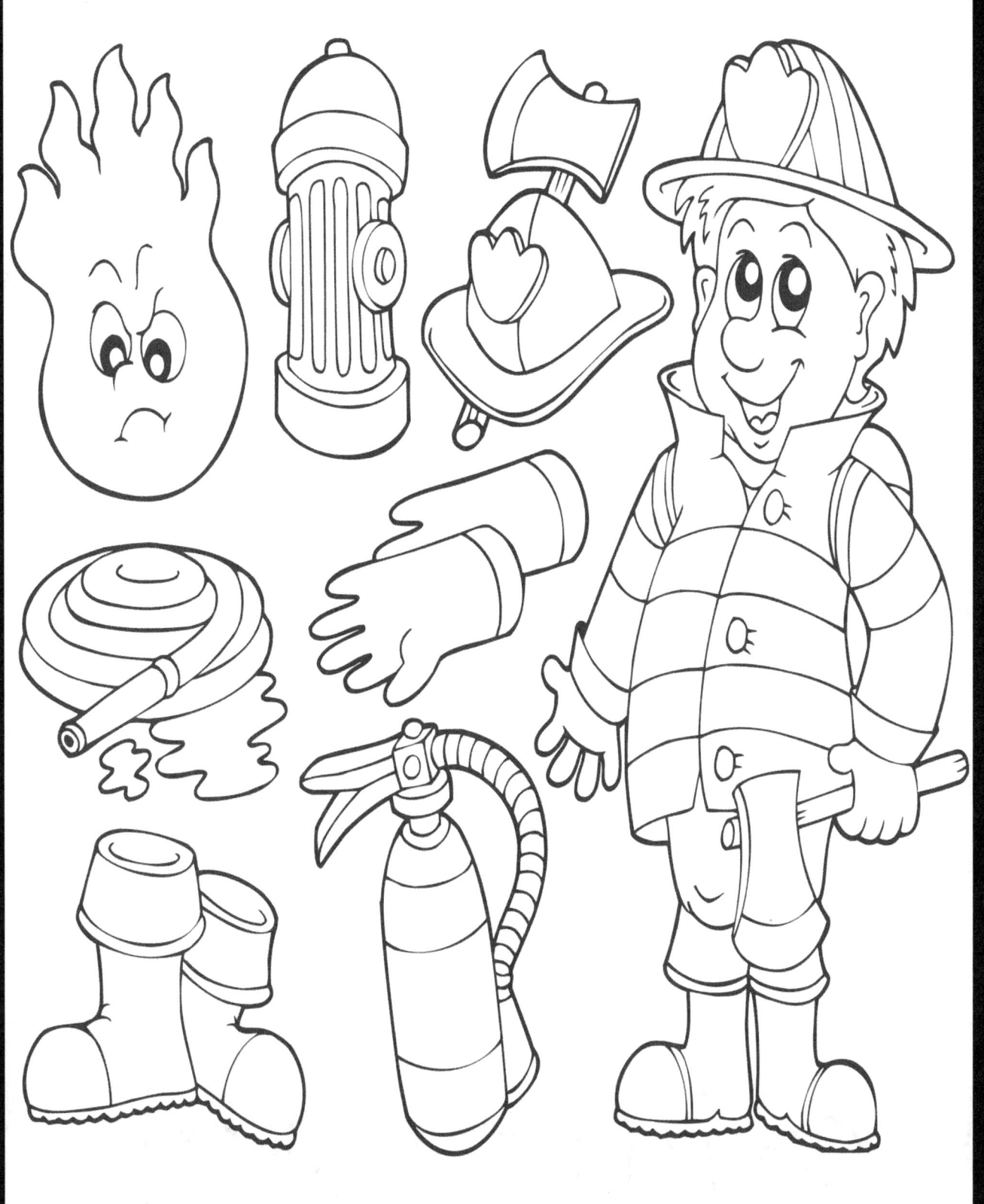

COLORING BOOK

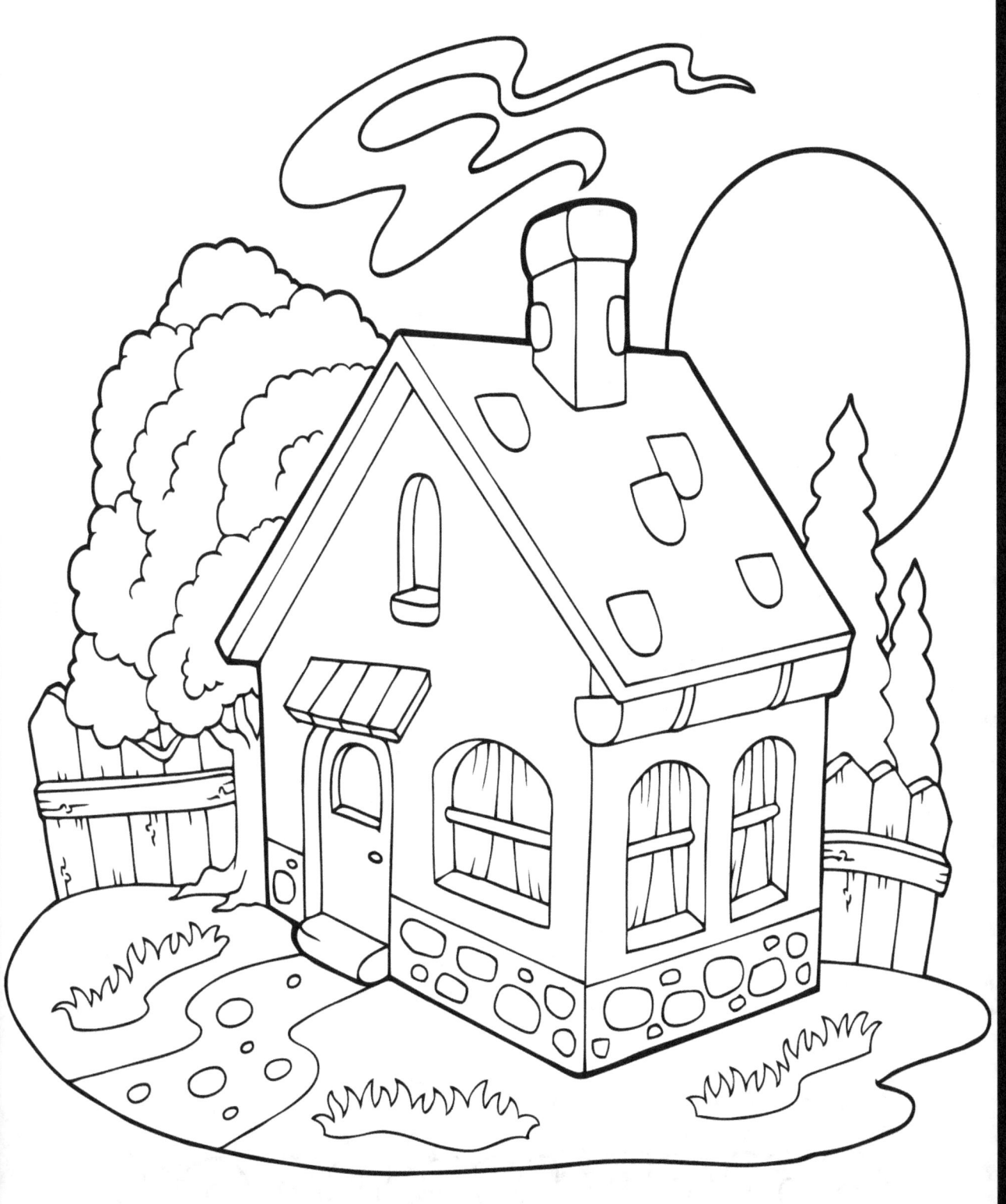

COLORING BOOK

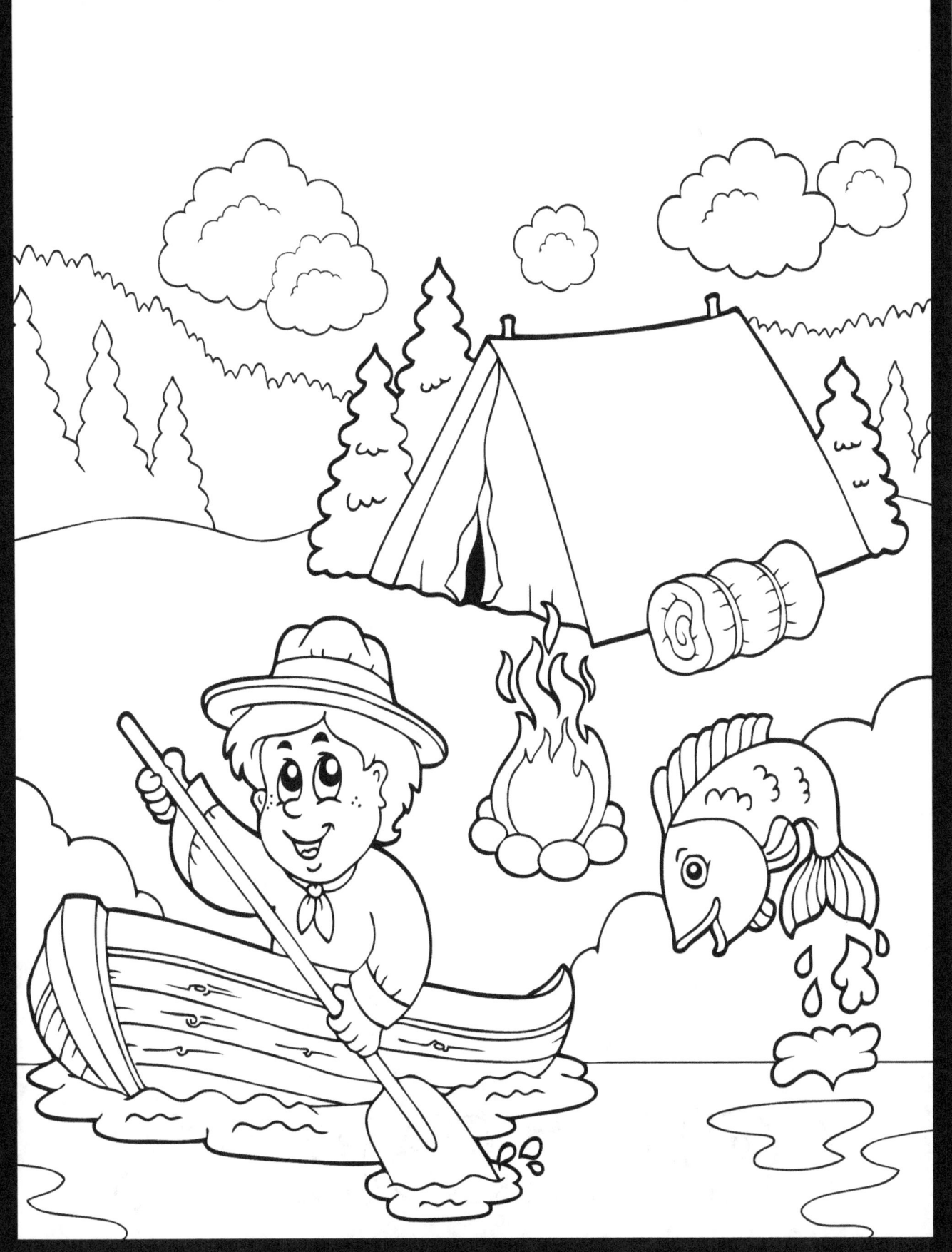

COLORING BOOK

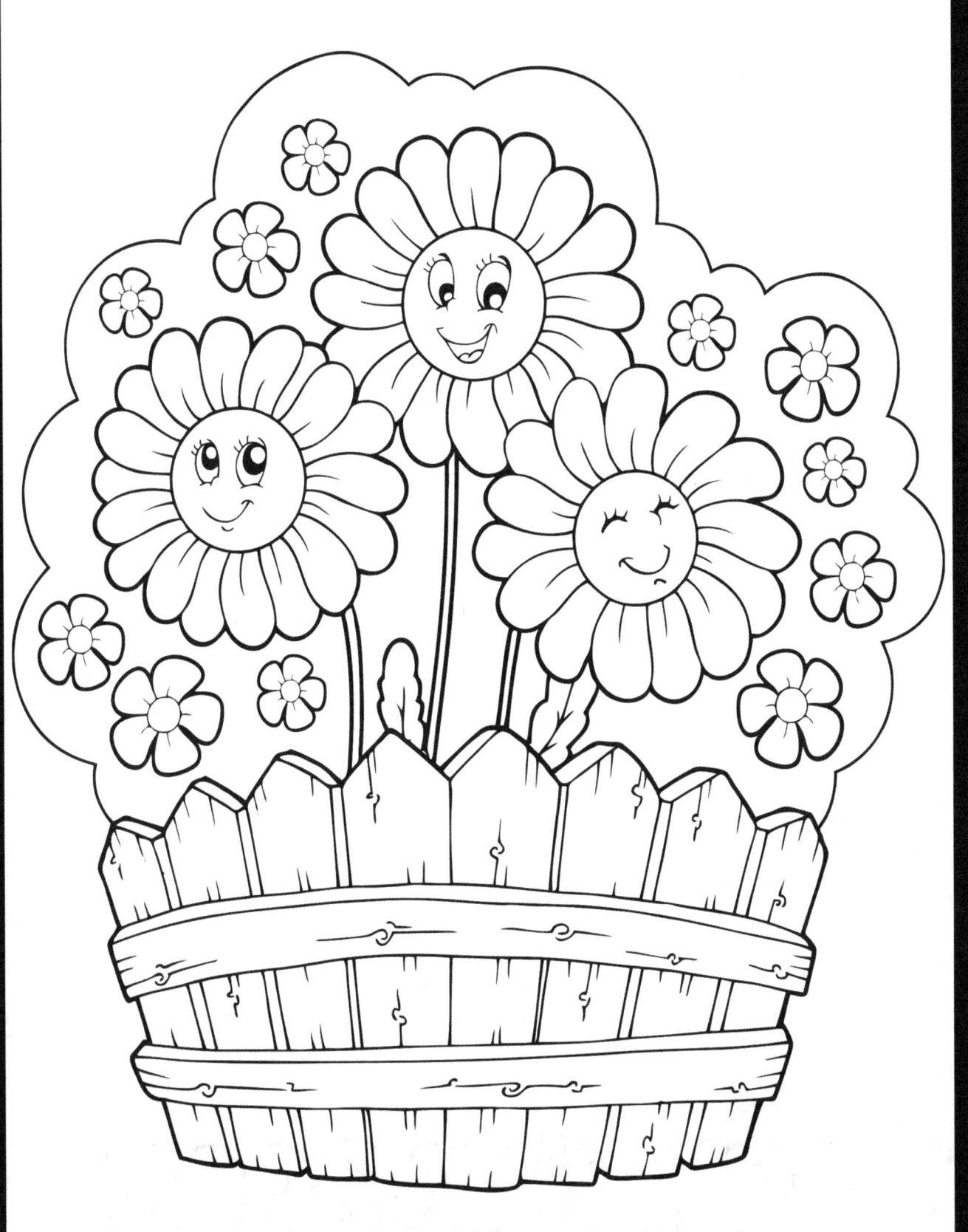

COLORING BOOK

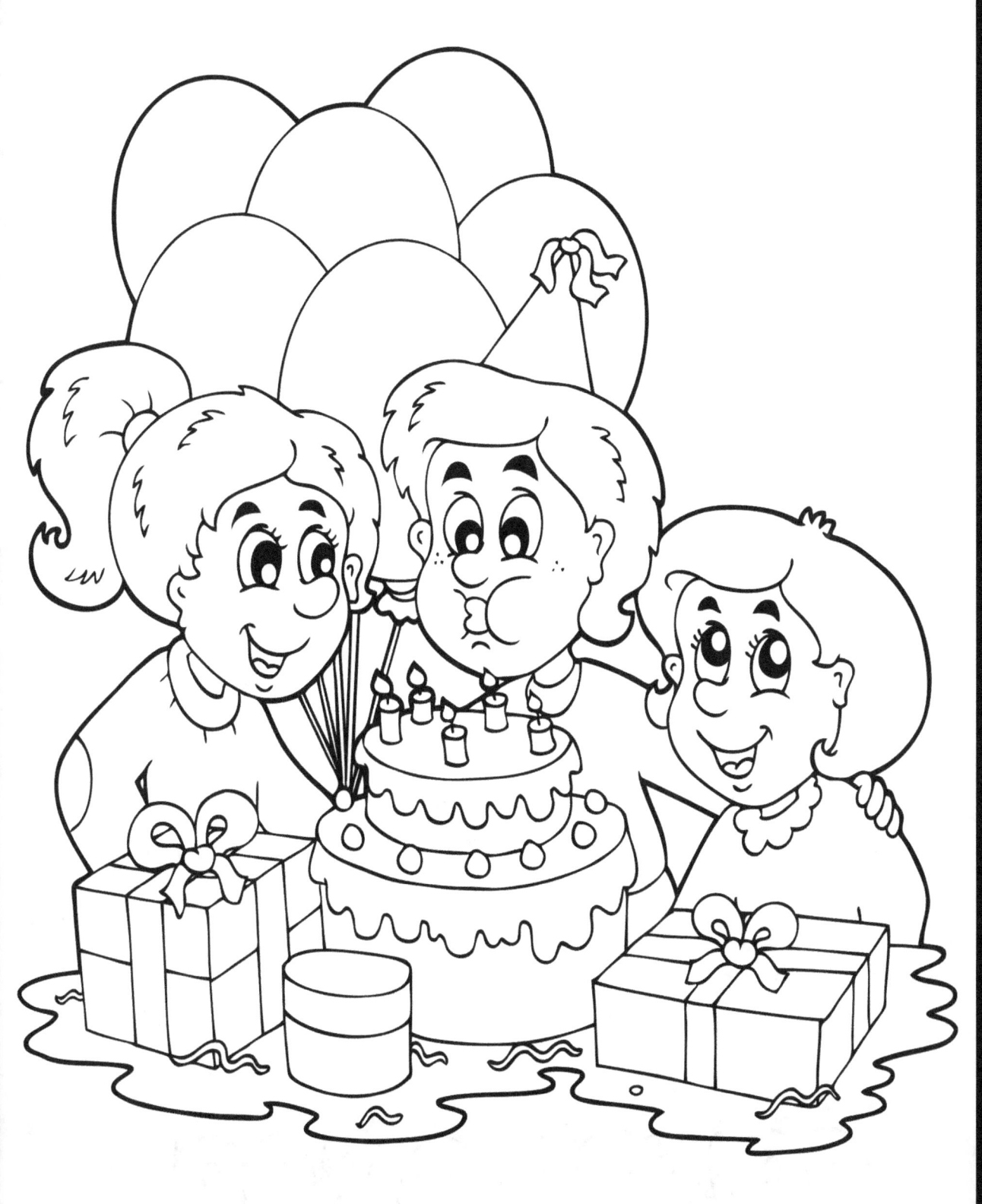

COLORING BOOK

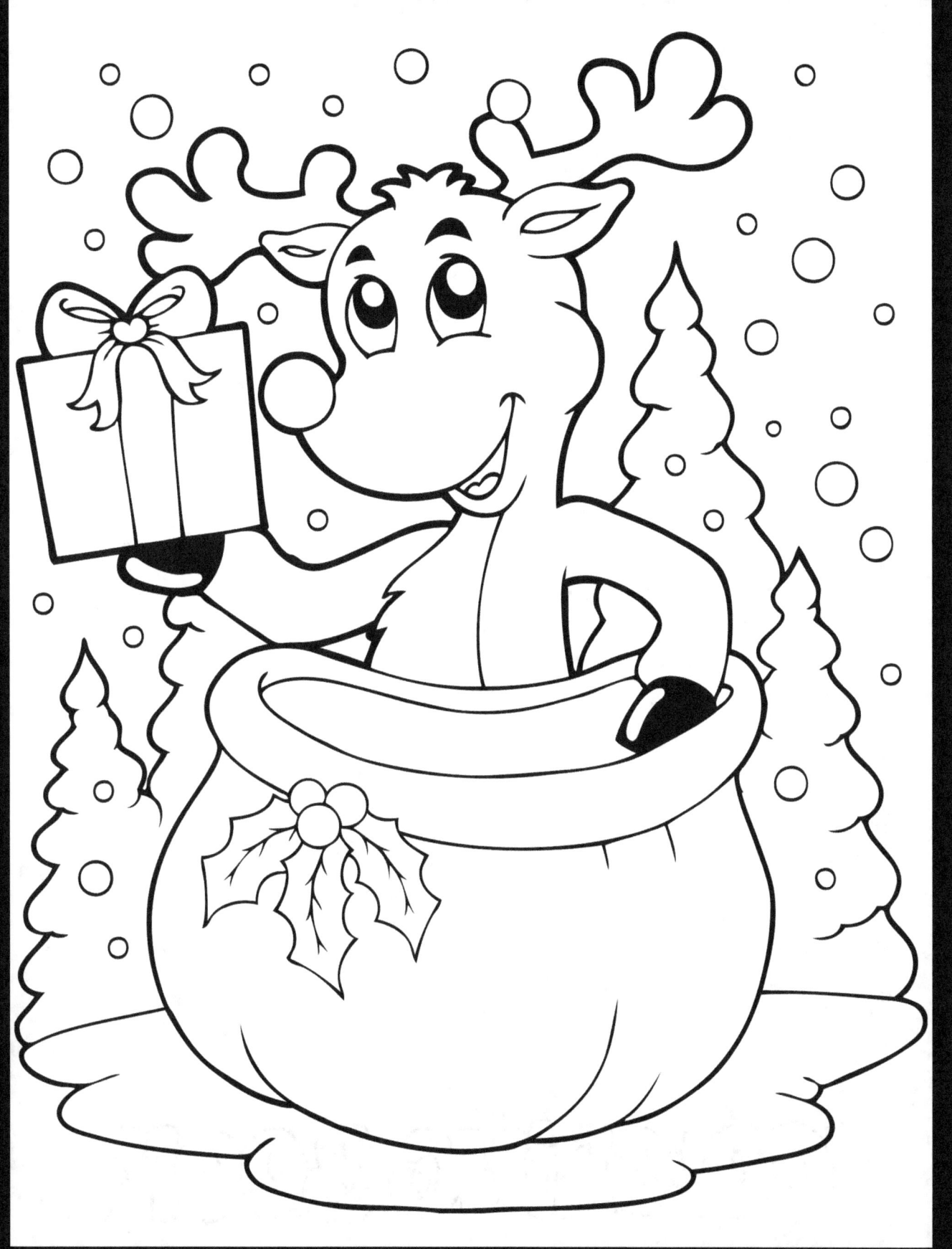

COLORING BOOK

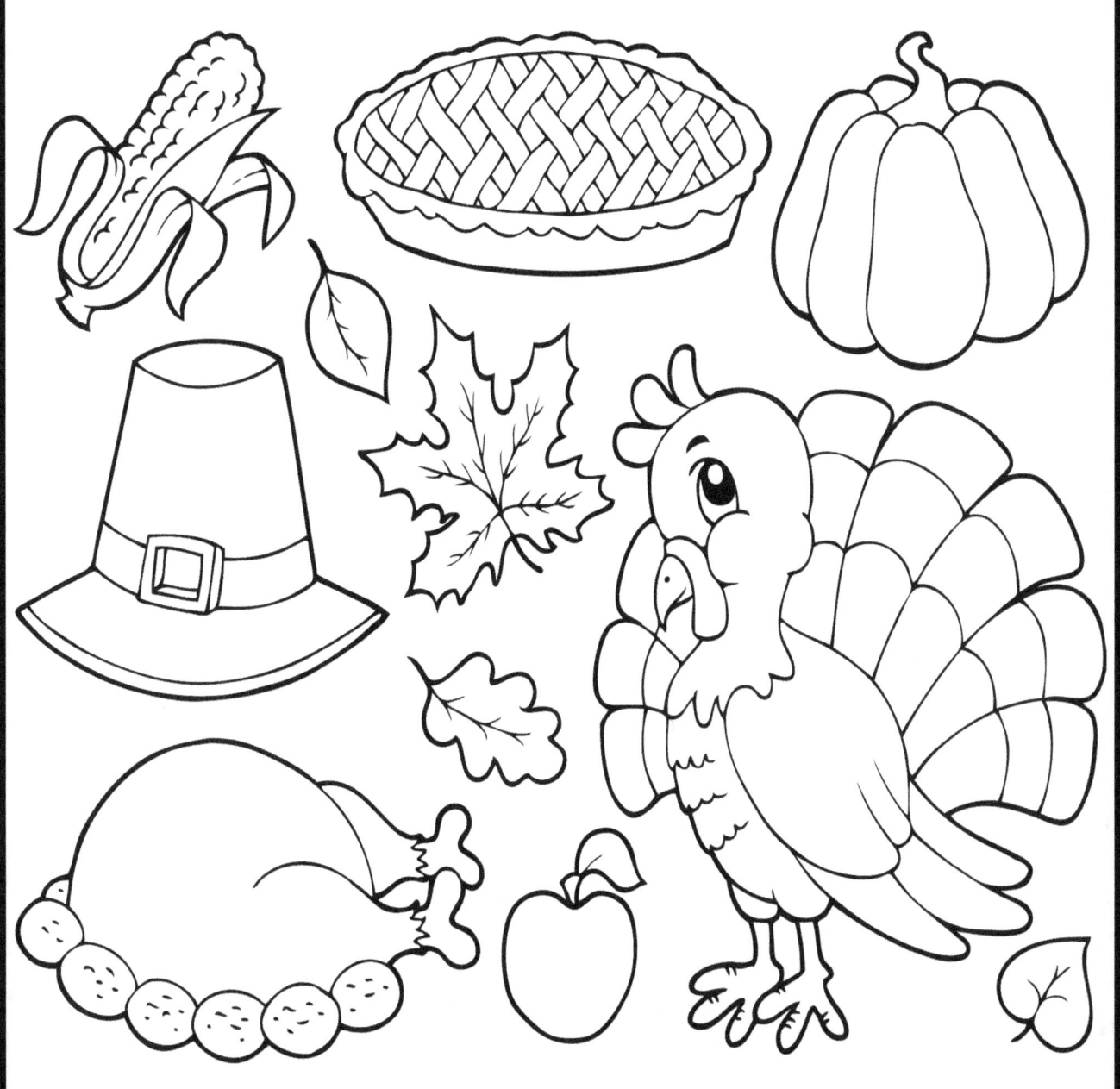

COLORING BOOK

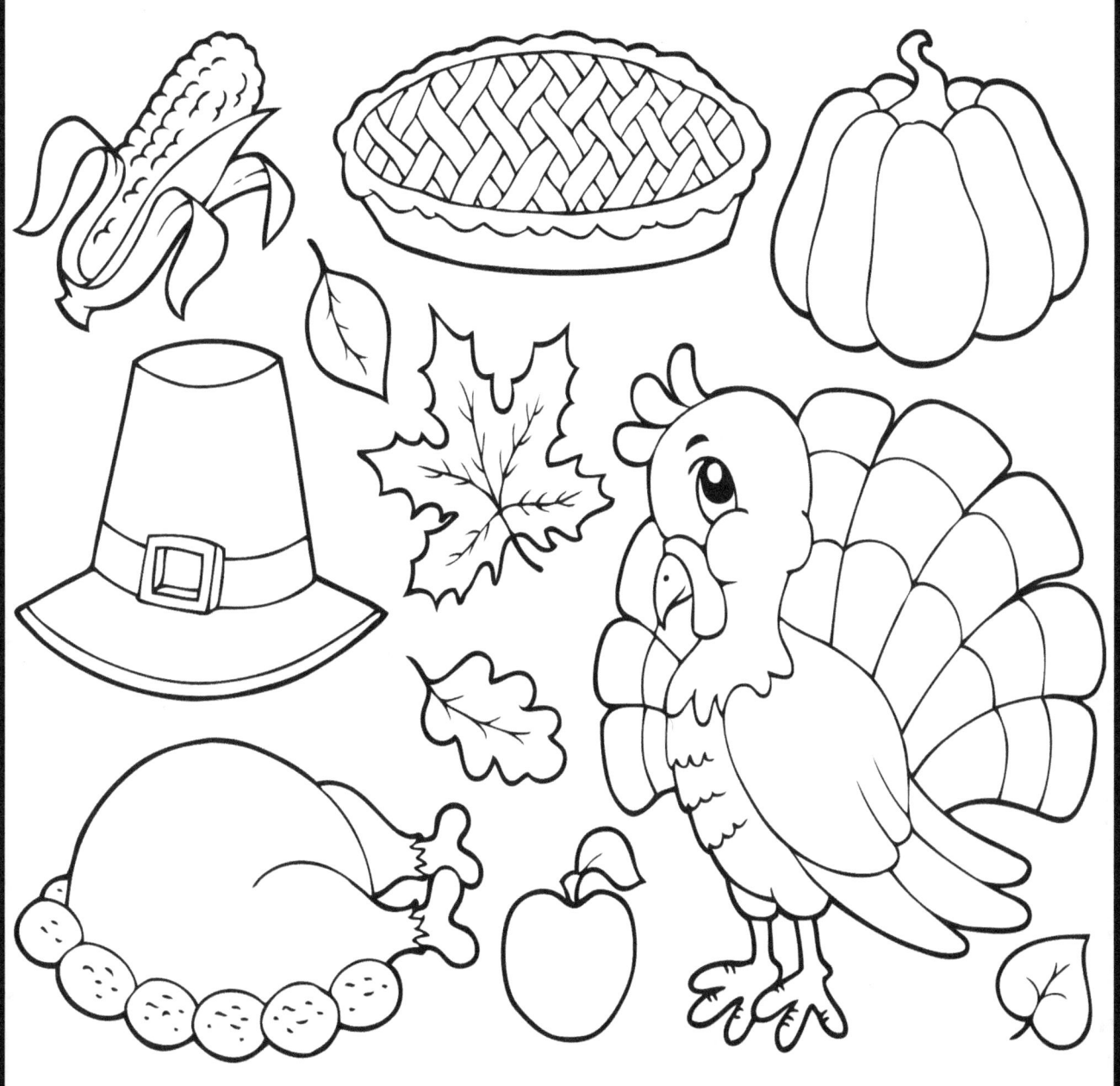

COLORING BOOK

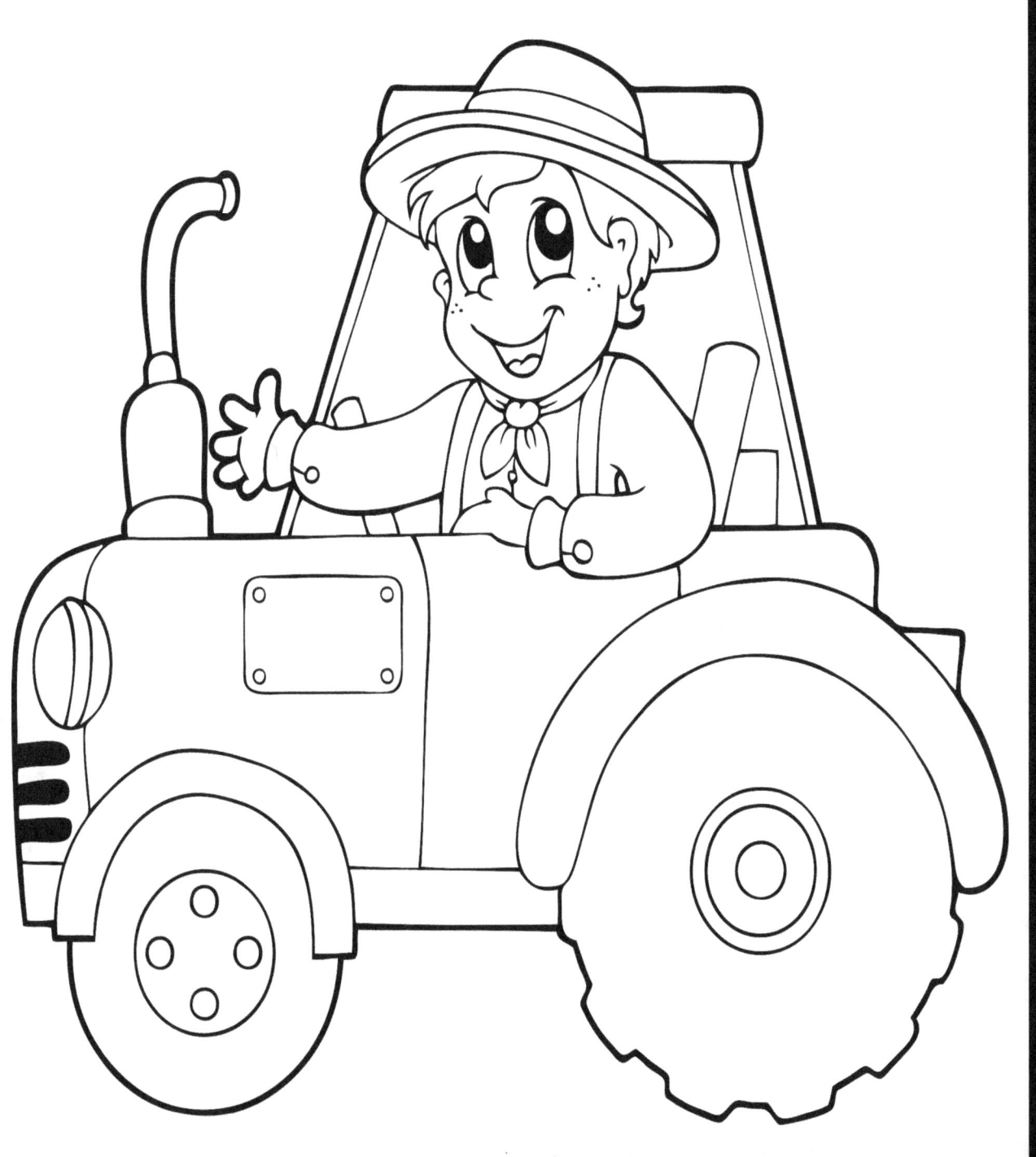

COLORING BOOK

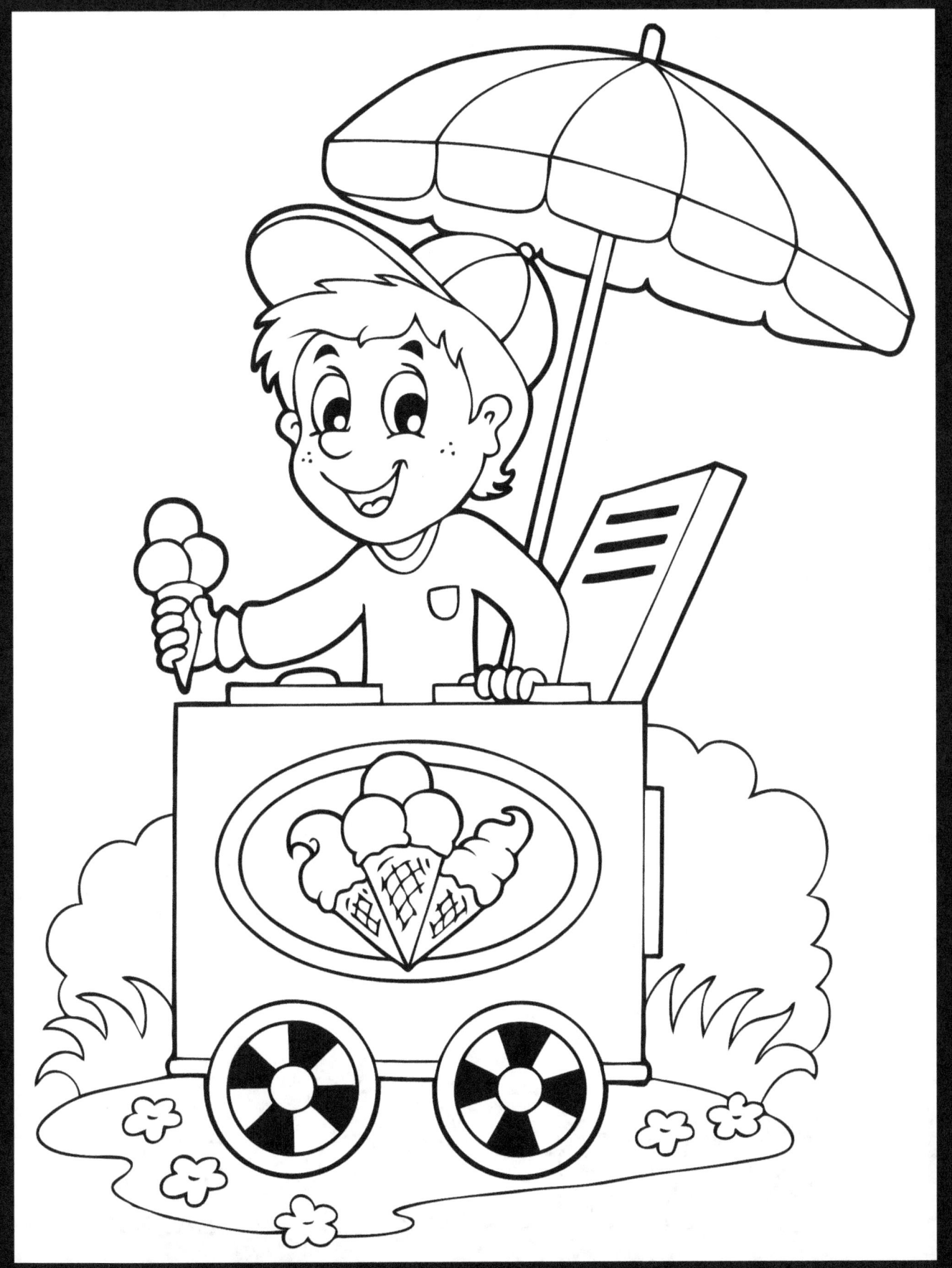

COLORING BOOK

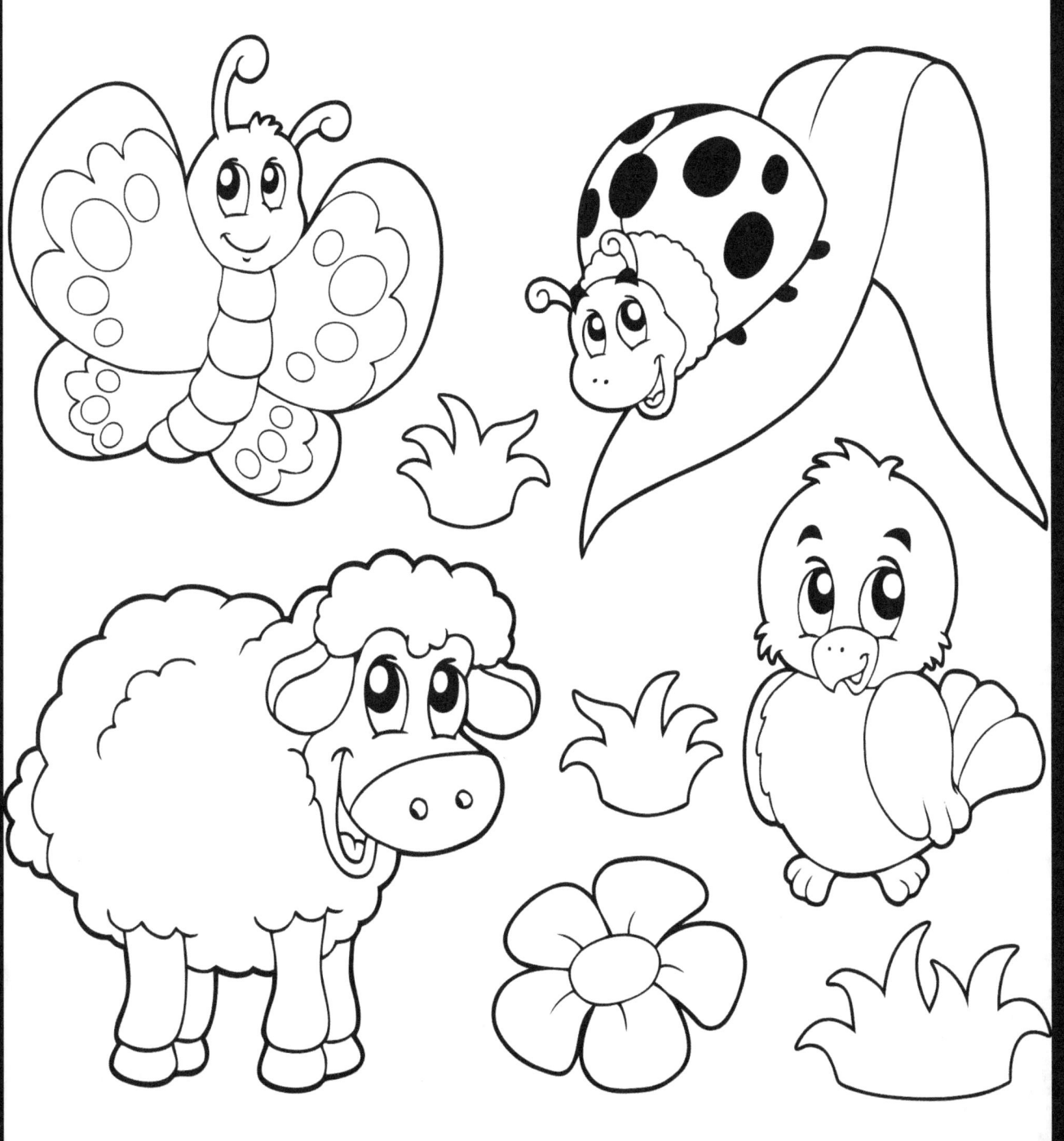

www.ingramcontent.com/pod-product-compliance
Lightning Source LLC
Chambersburg PA
CBHW080509220526

45465CB00006B/2424